THE VISION
OF THE TRINITY

George H. Tavard

University Press
of America™

BT
109
.T38

Acknowledgements

Thanks are due for authorization to quote copyrighted material, from The Collected Works of St John of the Cross translated by Kieran Kavanaugh and Otillo Rodriguez, copyright (c) 1964, 1979 by Washington Province of Discalced Carmelites, Inc. ICS Publications, 2131 Lincoln Road, N.E. Washington, D.C. 20002 U.S.A.

and also

from Meister Eckhart, tr. by Raymond Blackney, copyright 1957, by Harper & Row, Publishers, New York.

Abbreviations

The following abbreviations have been used:

C. O. D.: Conciliorum Oecumenicorum Decreta, Freiburg, 1962
D. - S.: Denzinger-Schönmetzer: Enchiridion Symbolorum, Definitionum et Declarationum, XXXII ed., Freiburg, 1963
P. L.: Migne: Patrologia Latina
S. Chr.: Sources Chrétiennes.

v

Foreword

The Anglican theologian Austin Farrer has presented revelation as an interplay of events and
images : "The great images (of the New Testament)
interpreted the events of Christ's ministry, death
and resurrection, and the events interpreted the
images; the interplay of the two is revelation.
Certainly the events without the images would be
no revelation at all, and the images without the
events would remain shadows in the clouds..." (The
Glass of Vision, London, 1958, p. 43). One may
find in this quotation the point of departure of
the present book, although, once launched, I have
followed a trajectory of my own: I have looked at
the doctrine of the Trinity as an image or vision,
and I have followed this vision and its development in the New Testament (chapter I); in the art,
especially of the early Church, the Middle Ages,
and the Oriental iconography (chapter II). Because
the theological approach to the doctrine of the
Trinity has been chiefly speculative, chapter III
looks at this speculative development, without, I
hope, losing sight of my prevailing visionary
focus. The vision of the Three is then studied as
it appears in the experience of several Christian
mystics, chosen for their representativeness of
the broad mystical tradition of orthodox Christianity (chapter IV). Chapter V attempts a contemporary Trinitarian synthesis, chiefly in the
light of the developing anthropological sciences;
pride of place is assigned to linguistics, in
keeping with my previous study of theological
method: La Théologie parmi les sciences humaines,
Paris, 1975.

The motif behind this exploration is simply the
conviction that the vision of the Three is central
to the Christian understanding of God and style of
living, and that the nucleus of contemporary theological research should be, not revision of past
positions for the sake of updating Christian
thought in the eyes of our contemporaries, and not
even human liberation, but God, as God is experi-

enced in Christian life and as this experience is or ought to be projected into theology.

What I have written here about the vision of the Three is complementary of what I have previously written about the Trinity, in Woman in Christian Tradition, Notre Dame, 1973, and A Way of Love, Maryknoll, N.Y., 1977. It confirms in a more strictly theological medium the vision embodied in my poetry: La Septième Vague, Paris, 1976, Song for Avalokita, Philadelphia, 1979, Le Silence d'une Demi-heure, Paris, 1980.

Methodist Theological School in Ohio
Delaware, Ohio

George H. Tavard

I

The Revealer

The picture of Jesus of Nazareth as recent New Testament scholarship tends to present it has little in common with the later formulation of the doctrines which are conveniently summed up in the expression, doctrine of the Trinity. The doctrinally-oriented episodes of the synoptic gospels are assigned to post-resurrection appearances; the post-resurrection appearances are traced back to imaginative reconstructions by the memory of the community. Thus the man Jesus is seen as a very unusual Jewish preacher who attempts a revolution in Jewish religion and is therefore condemned to death by the powers that be. This religious revolution touches directly the problem of the relations between God, called by Jesus with the endearing term, Abba,[1] and creatures. It does not seem to affect directly the conception of what God is in himself.

This general orientation of contemporary exegesis implies an unfortunate disregard of a major point. The questions that have traditionally found their answer in the doctrine of the Trinity are not abstract or speculative. And the traditional answers, for that matter, have not been philosophical. Discussion of what God is in himself is necessarily raised in Christianity by a basic fact: the religious experience, the sense of the numinous, the apprehension of the mysterium fascinosum et tremendum, the experience of God, acquire such peculiar features in Christian circles that the Jewish conception of the oneness of the One God - as embodied in the sch'ma Israel: "Hear, o Israel! The Lord is our God, the Lord alone!" (Deut. 6:4) - is felt to be inadequate. But if this was, as I expect to show in the next few pages, the experience of the disciples, and especially of Paul and of John, it would be surprising if it had not already been the experience of Jesus.

o o o

1

Even the most radical contemporary student of the synoptic gospels admits that, whatever obscurities surround the historical picture of Jesus, at least one thing is clear from the accounts of his life and ministry: Jesus must have had a very unique relation to God. The Jews who heard and saw him sensed this. Some went on to interpret it as sufficient warrant to follow him in such a kind of discipleship as no Old Testament prophet ever obtained from listeners and followers. Others were so shocked in their religious convictions and ways of thought that they felt bound to turn against him to the point of seeking his death. Few, if any, of those who heard and saw Jesus remained indifferent. At any rate, New Testament exegesis cannot settle alone the problem, what sort of relationship to God did Jesus experience? No adequate model for this relationship can be found in the obedience of prophets to their vocation, or in the devotion of priests to their cultic ritual, or in the devotional fervor of the "poor of the Lord", or in the painstaking devotion to Torah which was common among the Pharisees, or in the asceticism of the Essenes, or in the eager expectation of the age to come which pervades apocalyptic literature. The synoptic gospels, and still more the gospel of John, present a picture of what must be, in the entire history of the Hebrews and the Jews, a unique case, an ephapax, without precedent, and without the possibility of later duplication. Jesus fits all sorts of categories in the external events of his life: he is a preacher, a prophet, a student of Torah, the head of a group of "poor of the Lord", a miracle-worker, a healer of the sick and the possessed, a spiritual revolutionary. But in order to depict his interior life the evangelists insist on two points, which are both uncommon in the Jewish literature of the times: the importance of his private prayer, and the title which he often applies to God.

The title, Abba, expresses, in the Aramaic of the times, the close relationship of a child to his father in an endearing way similar to the

2

English usage of the word, dad or daddy. This is entirely new in Jewish literature, although we have no way of knowing if it was not an accepted term in the spoken language of Galilee. In any case the disciples of Jesus do not seem to employ this term. It appears twice in the epistles of Paul; and in both cases (Gal. 4:6 and Rom. 8:15) it suggests the intimate action of the Spirit who makes us pray "Abba, Father", that is, who incor-porates the faithful into Jesus's relationship to the one whom Jesus called, Abba. Yet Paul avoids the word in the many doxologies of his epistles. As far as one can tell, the word was not carried into the liturgies of the early Church. Or, if it may have belonged to some of the earliest litur-gies, it did not survive into those of the second century. Neither the Didachè nor the liturgy of St Justin or the later but presumably conservative liturgy of Hippolytus contain the term. In both Greek and Latin, the standard formal word, Father, expresses the Christian's relatic to God; and this is also the word used in homilies and commen-taries to speak of Jesus's relation to his Father. The use of Abba to pray to God is equally unknown in post-Christian rabbinic literature.

One is therefore entitled to see this word as special to Jesus. It undoubtedly goes back to what the earliest disciples remembered of his life on earth before his death and rising. The problem therefore becomes one of interpreting its implica-tions. And it would seem that, by and large, New Testament scholarship has not faced the basic question which is implied in Jesus's puzzling use of this word. It is customary in contemporary writing to see this term as an outstanding expres-sion of Jesus's independence of thought, boldness of expression, freedom from precedent. Not only is Jesus free in regard to the institutional authorities and the traditional regulations of Judaism. Not only is he able, when he wants, to disregard both Jewish hierarchy and Roman power; not only does he ignore or even contradict Saddu-cean traditionalism and the Pharisees' progressive interpretations of Torah; not only does he keep his distances from the Zealots' underground preparations for a future messianic struggle for power, and from the otherworldly asceticism of John the Baptist or of the monks of Qumran: Jesus shows himself free even in regard to the prophetic tradition by depicting God, not under the impressive figure of a heavenly Shekinah as described by the prophet Ezechiel, 1:4-28, but with the image of one's own daddy. Jesus's piety is not in the line of the Merkabah mysticism in which Jewish scholarship sees the main type of mystical experience in Judaism, or of the esoteric speculations of medieval hasidism and of the later Kabbalah; it belongs more in the spirit of the eighteenth century hasidism of the Baal Shem.[2] Yet even the hasidim will not emulate Jesus's familiarity with God. There was no precedent for calling God Abba; there has been no follow up. Jesus owes nothing to anyone as far as his relation to God is concerned. No one, Jew or Christian, has been able to borrow his language to speak to God or to speak of God. Thus Jesus may be seen as the ideal model for the Christian who, as Luther formulated it perceptively, "is a perfectly free lord of all, subject to none", while being at the same time, "perfectly obedient servant of all, subject to all."[3] Jesus, obedient unto death, remains yet totally free. Justification is neither by law, be this the inspired Torah or the inspired New Testament, nor by the invocation of the classical names of God or even by awesome respect for God's unpronounceable name. It is by the faith which, inspired in their hearts by the Spirit, relates each of the disciples to God in a new way which owes nothing to systematic forms, rites or personal behavior, but which is indebted only to the very freedom of God manifested in Jesus. Thus the uniqueness of Jesus's title for God may suggest enlightening conclusions for the Christian life.

Yet it seems that a still more important point is at stake. If Abba is the word which best expresses Jesus's relationship to God, this implies at least that the traditional Hebrew designations for God are not adequate to his experience. The old tribal names of God - of which Yahweh was the most prominent before it came so to designate the transcendence of God that it should not be pronounced - are not adequate, not only because some of them have become archaic, but also because they imply a nationalistic claim on exclusive knowledge of the true name of God. In the usage at the time of Jesus, Yahweh has become a liturgical title reserved to the annual rites of Yom Kippour; pronunciation of it is reserved to the High Priest who has entered the Holy of Holies. Other older names, such as El, El shaddai, Elohim, may express the common relation to God of all creatures, but are insufficient to express Jesus's own experience. More recent names, such as Adonai (Lord), Dabar (Word), seem more attuned to the general experience of Israel as the People of the Lord, as the People to whom God has spoken. Yet they do not express what is special to Jesus. Unfortunately, what is special to Jesus cannot really be conceptualized and formulated in any other language than his own as used by himself. We can merely suggest that one has to turn to later Trinitarian theology in order to grasp the proper implications of Jesus's denomination of God as Abba. The one whom Jesus called Abba cannot be the Elohim or the Yahweh of the Hebraic tradition nor the Adonai or Dabar of more recent Jewish tradition. Jesus cannot relate to this God in prayer - except in the largely formal use of official titles in the institutionalized prayer of the Temple or of the Synagogue - for the simple and at the same time fantastic reason that one does not pray to oneself. Jesus does not pray to Elohim because he is too close to Elohim, so close that later Christian reflection will conclude that they are, in a sense that needs careful explanation, identical. Yet Jesus, in his parables, teaches, reveals new things about Elohim and especially the one basic point that Elohim is truly not as the Judaism of his time imagines.

Jesus relates to Abba, not as to what all religions, including that of the Old Testament, have called God or the Divinity. Rather, when

5

Jesus prays, Abba, he speaks from within the Divinity itself, addressing the one whom later Christian theology will regard exclusively as the Father. Admittedly, it is only in the light of later Trinitarian theology that such a conclusion can be reached. But it does not imply an undue reading back of Trinitarian theology into the New Testament. Jesus did not reveal God only by talking about God. He revealed God by being what he himself was, in his life, his death and his rising from the dead. And what Jesus was did not, could not, fully appear even to his closest disciples, even when these had become convinced that he was not among the dead but had been made, beyond death, the supreme embodiment of life. Jesus did not reveal the doctrine of the Trinity. What he revealed was that God, to him, was what God was to no one else: not Yahweh, not Elohim, not Adonai, not Dabar, but Abba. And I take it to be Paul's meaning in Galatians and Romans: if the Spirit in us cries, "Abba, Father," this is not a common experience, and may not even be the experience of all. To realise that "the Spirit of the Son" cries "Abba, Father," within us, we need a particularly profound union to Jesus, so profound that we somehow, obscurely, feel what he himself experienced fully - the divine Filiation.

o o o

That Jesus did not proclaim himself the Messiah, that he even eschewed any such suggestion, is largely accepted in contemporary scholarship. Whatever Messianism later christology attributed to Jesus could only have been implicit in his actions and his life. But exegesis has not sufficiently fathomed the reason behind the silence of Jesus about himself. Yet the reason is simple enough. Messianism in the broad sense corresponds, not only to the popular conception of a royal Messiah with a political and religious mission of liberation, but also to diverse strains of the Jewish expectation of a new age. Self-identification with a Messiah is possible on one condition: the Messiah must be conceived, and his mission ex-

6

pressed, in the terms of everyday life which furnish the language of our thoughts. Jesus could be, and could know he was, the Messiah, just as others have thought they were. If he experienced in himself a call to a specific function at a given time in a certain place, he could have said he was the Messiah, and he could have let his disciples believe it. Indeed, it would have helped him to let it be known, at least to the group of his close followers.

But it is not possible to show oneself as the Messiah, or as the new David, or as the New Moses, or as Elias redivivus, or as the Prophet, or even as the apocalyptic Son of Man,[4] if one's most basic experience of self escapes all these categories and all other culture-bound ways of thought. If Jesus's identity is that, whatever he may be as a Galilean from Nazareth, he is above all Divine Son, what he is to himself belongs to the ineffable. It is not communicable, since any one who would claim such a Filiation could not be believed. Neither nature nor culture have developed the proper categories for such an experience. What Jesus is to himself in his most intimate experience of God, he cannot even know with conceptual knowledge, for humanity has no concepts for it. Whenever the development of culture has produced concepts that approximate to such an experience, it has had to stop short. It has provided symbols, images, icons, myths of divine relationship which, poorly grasped in ordinary human experience, have been interpreted in idolatrous ways. Or it has taken refuge in the silence of the Upanishads. Or, reversing the affirmative movement of self-identification, it has found another refuge in negation, seeing the ultimate reality of all as absolute void.

What Jesus was to himself appears occasionally in the gospels, though only indirectly and by implication. No one in the entire Old Testament had ever reversed Torah. Even the prophets, who were responsible for a great leap forward in the religious sensitivity of Israel, had modified the

7

understanding of the Law without contradicting the Law.   Ezechiel had taught individual responsibility (Ez. 18), but he had not abolished corporate responsibility.   An unknown psalmist had proclaimed in Ps. 50 that the true sacrifice is the sacrifice of praise, but he had not advocated the abolition of traditional holocausts in the Temple.   Jesus alone does what no one has yet dared to do.   He allows the disciples to perform actions that are not permitted on the Sabbath (Mk 2:23-3:5).   In the sayings that we call the sermon on the mount, Jesus alters some of the commands of the Law: "You have heard the commandment imposed on your forefathers...What I say to you is..." (Matt. 5:21-22).   In the case of divorce he contradicts the respected book of Deuteronomy, calling adulterer the man who follows the regulations of Deut. 24:1-4 to repudiate his wife.

Is this blasphemy, as the Sadducees, staunch defenders of the pure Torah, were led to conclude? Is it an unbelievable hybris, an insane megalomania, as the pious Pharisees were inclined to think?   Is it the idiosyncrasy of a sectarian leader eager to create his own type of Judaism, somewhat parallel to, while different from, the Qumran monastic ethics?   Is it not rather the normal and natural behavior of one who is above Torah because he is himself the initiator of Torah? The Jewish understanding of the prophecies never suggested that the Messiah would rewrite the Law. That the legate of God would inscribe a new law in the heart, inaugurate a new covenant, was commonplace among the prophets of Israel.   But this was taken to mean that the Messiah would bring about the heartfelt fidelity to the Law which Israel had always hankered for, yet been unable to achieve.   Paul himself in his letters justifies the setting aside of the Law with obscure midrashic reasonings which scarcely conceal his embarrassment at doing what he nonetheless feels he has to do.   But the gospels record no such embarrassment in Jesus.   On the contrary, they report popular astonishment at the authority with which he spoke. It was Jesus's natural behavior to over-

8

come the Law when the Law became outmoded by being confronted with himself. If Jesus does not say who is he, if the very conditions of human thought make it impossible for him to conceptualize who he is, he acts according to who he is, the maker, and therefore also the unmaker, of Torah.

o o o

In these conditions, it is not surprising that Jesus' preaching, as it has come down to us in the synoptic gospels, is focused on the idea of the kingdom. In the Greek of the New Testament, this is called the kingdom of God but also the kingdom of heaven, especially in the very semitic gospel of Matthew.[5]   Some of the modern translations prefer the word Reign, to Kingdom. But this is misleading. For, granted that the letter of the text can be rendered indifferently as kingdom and as reign, the connotations of the two words are notably different. It is my contention here that Jesus is not primarily interested in preaching power or dominion, as implied in the word, reign, be that the power and the dominion of God. Nor is he eager to confront his listeners with a conundrum out of which they can escape only through an existential decision here and now. Rather, Jesus preaches another realm than the visible earth, another city - to use Augustine's phrase - than this earthly city, another Jerusalem than the one where David established his capital and where Herod the Great recently built the second Temple. This realm or kingdom is properly indescribable, ineffable; it cannot be conceptualized or imagined; it can be hinted at, designated obliquely and indirectly. For these reasons it is spoken of in parables. In the method of parabolic telling, the story told, the event reported, the behavior described pertain to ordinary human life; yet they also have a mythical dimension which, to those who have ears to hear, reveals the kingdom. To others, the parable remains a nice story, or an astonishing paradox, or an impertinent discourse.

o o o

9

Unlike other prophets, Jesus does not narrate parables about the politics of Israel. Unlike diverse founders of religions or initiators of religious revivals, he does not propose parables about the origins of the cosmos or the destinies of humankind. The apocalyptic passages of Mk 13, Matt. 24, Lk. 12, 17 and 21 must have been considerably inflated in their early transmission, presumably in an effort to interpret some sayings of Jesus about the Son of Man.

The expression, basileia tou theou, ascribes the kingdom to "the God", the One who, in hellenistic thought, would be the Absolute, the Highest God, carefully distinguished from all that may be called divine in a subordinate or appropriated sense. Throughout their history, the Hebrews had invoked the Absolute as Elohim, whose personal name, revealed to the Hebraic nation alone, was believed to be Yahweh, and for whom they had devised other appellations, since Yahwah was deemed too sacred a name to be pronounced. Uttering the name would have amounted to claiming somehow to see God. The expression, o theos, was no doubt understood in the same way by the evangelists themselves, insofar as their thinking was not yet fully Trinitarian. It was their designation for Yahweh, whom they took to be, in keeping with the Jewish context of early Christian thought, not only the only God there is but also all that there is of God.

In the beginning of Trinitarian thinking which is adumbrated in the later sections of the New Testament, the kingdom would be the kingdom of the Father, of the One who alone is o theos in the strict sense because he is the unbegotten, the originator, the ultimate principle of the Divinity. But the perspective of Jesus had to be different. The Kingdom of Elohim, the kingdom of the heavens must have, as it were, two levels. As the kingdom of Abba, it belongs to the One who is beyond Yahweh-Elohim, whom the Jewish hearers of Jesus did not know because he was yet unrevealed in their life. Into this kingdom no one can enter

10

except the Son, who comes from it without having left it. In the mouth of Jesus, the parables of the kingdom reveal first of all that there exists a realm so far unsuspected, an impenetrable aura of divinity, which no one has ever entered since no one can see the God and live, yet of which he, Jesus, can speak, since he belongs to it, comes from it, and soon will return to it. But Jesus cannot describe it, cannot even conceptualize it, because no words in any language can formulate the experience of being the Son. There is, accordingly, another level of the myth: the kingdom of Elohim, of which Jesus speaks, is the kingdom of himself, of which he is the king, an aura of Divinity around Jesus closely related to what the Old Testament had called the Spirit of God. This is the kingdom of the One whom the gospel of John calls the logos, whom Paul calls the kyrios, of the One who gave the Law, who spoke in the prophets, who sent the Apostles. Thus the parables of the kingdom are Jesus's mythical presentation of himself and of his mission on earth. To say that Jesus has a kingdom is, on the analogy of the Old Testament, to imply that he has a Spirit, that this Spirit seeks those who belong to Jesus and brings them into his joy.

o o o

This meaning of the kingdom and of the implications of Jesus's name for his Father, Abba, may help us interpret further the Trinitarian import of the resurrection of Jesus, as it is reported in the gospels. Undoubtedly, the resurrection is the major event in Jesus's revelation of the divine life. For it is due to the apostles' new perception of the mystery of Jesus that they began to understand what he had been all along, and which they had hitherto been unable to grasp.

What then was the post-resurrection experience of the disciples?

Recent discussions about the materiality of the return of Jesus from the dead and about the historicity of the story of the empty tomb have tended to hide the center of the resurrection message. It is self-evident that any report about Jesus having risen required at least from common sense that the disciples had to check the matter of the tomb: if the tomb was not empty, then whatever had shaken the early witnesses of the risen Jesus must be given another explanation than his rising. Contemporary philosophical reflection, along the lines of the phenomenology of Merleau-Ponty, happens to converge on the hebraic identification of personality, not with a soul whose presence in a body is more or less accidental (as Greek philosophy saw it), but with the totality of "the flesh". The person is not distinct from the body, which serves as the only locus of experience and as the only medium of expression and communication of the person. The authors of the New Testament translated this semitic conception into Greek with the help of the term, sarx. Because this word designated the flesh rather than the body (soma), and was already used to mean something like the human condition, it could more easily be semantically slanted toward the hebraic conception of the human totality. Rather than an edifice with several levels distinguished by the Greeks - such as soma, psyche, nous - man is an integral whole that cannot be divided into hierarchic levels. For the Greeks, the nous or soul survives when the body dies. For the older Hebrews, the whole flesh (nephesh) goes down into she'ol where it vegetates in the diminished existence of the dead. With the Pharisaic school of thought, the flesh, however, is destined to an ultimate resurrection, the details of which are unclear.

It is precisely in relation to this Pharisaic hope in the resurrection of the flesh that Paul presents the rising of Christ from the dead as "the first fruits of those who have fallen asleep" (1 Cor. 15:20). This determines the first pole of the Pauline message: the rising of Jesus is central to the Christian faith, which looks forward to the resurrection of the dead. But there is a second pole to Paul's teaching on the rising of Jesus. Although the risen Jesus manifested himself to "Cephas, then to the Twelve", then to "five hundred brothers at once", then to James, then to all the apostles, and last of all to Paul (1 Cor.,15:5-8), it was not in what we call the body that Jesus was seen. The polemic of 1 Cor. 15:35-58 is directed precisely against some of the brothers who are anxious about the body in which they will be raised. These presumably are Greek Christians who normally think in terms of body, psyche, and soul rather than with the semitic conception of the flesh. To them Paul insists that the risen body is a "heavenly body", a "spiritual body", (1 Cor., 15:40;44) patterned on "the heavenly man" (1 Cor., 15:48) who is no other than Jesus risen from the dead. It is therefore not in the body (in the Greek sense) although it is in the flesh (in the Hebraic sense) that Jesus reveals himself after rising from the dead. He makes himself present and he is seen in his lordship (1 Cor. 9:1). When Paul also writes: "The Lord is the Spirit" (2 Cor., 3:17), he insists that the risen Jesus is not a <u>soma</u>, a body. His rising is not a clinical ressuscitation, but a spiritual event by which his <u>sarx</u>, his flesh, becomes <u>pneuma</u>, spirit. And therefore, in Rom. 1:3-4, the resurrection is the manifestation, as "Son of God with power in the Spirit of holiness," of the one who is already "his Son, born of the line of David in the flesh". Jesus, already known in the flesh, is now seen to be also power in the Spirit. His rising from the dead thus shows him to have a unique relationship to his Father and to the divine Spirit.

Had Paul been an ordinary rabbi, he presumably would have stopped here. Having affirmed that the Messiah had arrived and been crowned by God, he would have felt no need to depart radically from the basic Jewish faith in the One God. But Paul perceived much more in the Jesus who came to him, on the way to Damascus, in the form of the Son of Man, and through whose Spirit he felt himself guided at some key points in his ministry. The

13

rising of Jesus has a two fold aspect: it marks
the arrival of the man Jesus at the goal set to
him by the Spirit, and it is the return of Jesus
as Spirit to the dignity which belonged to him in
the first place. This is presumably the background behind the remarkable expression of Phil.
2:6-11: "Though he was in the form of God, he did
not deem equality to God something to be grasped
at..." The "form of God" (morphe theou) has connotations deriving from the Greek esthetic tradition. The beauty of a statue does not reside in
its outward shape, in the lines and proportions
of its parts, in their integration into a harmo-
nious whole; these outward aspects of art have the
ultimate purpose of conveying to the onlooker the
inner spiritual reality of the model. Behind
everything that is empirically experienced there
is also, in the Platonic tradition, a heavenly
pattern whose spiritual "form" is imaged in the
visible shape. The heavenly pattern of which
Jesus the Christ is the faithful image, however,
is unlike all other spiritual models: it is the
very "form of God", the divine beauty. Being "in
the form of God", Jesus is equal to God. But this
equality is not a privilege that needs protecting
and preserving. Being his very own by birthright,
it is not in danger of being lost if it is shared,
to the extent that it can possibly be shared. In
order to share it, Christ has also taken on himself the "form of the servant". What Paul teaches
in this letter is repeated in a slightly different
vocabulary in the letter to the Colossians(whether
of strictly Pauline authorship or not): "He is
the image of the invisible God..." (Col. 1:15).
The image, the icon, is the visibility among us
of the invisible form of God. That Jesus the
Christ is also called, in Colossians, "the first-
born of every creature," does not make him a creature: rather, he is the medium of all creation.
"All has been created by him and for him". He is
therefore "the Beginning." By his resurrection
he is "the first born from among the dead." And
just as the hymn of Philippians ends with the proclamation that Jesus Christ "is Lord, to the glory
of God the Father" (Phil. 2:11), this passage of

14

Colossians sees the climax of the relationship between God and Jesus in that "God was pleased to make the _Pleroma_ dwell in him" (Col. 1:19). Jesus "must have primacy in all things" (Col. 1:18). For the unique relationship of Jesus to God in this life is the image, the visible form, of an invisible relationship to God in the form of God itself, which is previous, simultaneous and posterior to his own life on earth.

o o o

A similar conclusion follows from a careful reading of the resurrection accounts in the synoptic gospels, if at least these accounts are not isolated from the rest of the gospels. For the sobriety of the evangelists about the manner in which the risen Jesus shows himself to the women and to the apostles does not betray on their part hesitancy or ignorance about the post-resurrection experience. In fact, they need not describe the risen Jesus because they already have done so. In their faith, Mark, Matthew, Luke knew that what Jesus showed himself to be after rising from the dead, he already was. And this they had already depicted in two major events placed during the ministry of Jesus: his baptism by John and his transfiguration. These major theophanies should be understood as post-resurrection interpretations of pre-resurrection happenings, although, in the case of the transfiguration, it is impossible to imagine what this happening could have been. These are of course the main Trinitarian images of the gospels: in the light of the resurrection, the disciples, interpreted by the evangelists, understood that Jesus was, even before he died, the beloved Son-Servant of his _Abba_ and the chief recipient of the divine Spirit. The voice from heaven suddenly breaks the prophetic silence in which _Elohim_ had enshrouded himself since the waning of prophecy. Even John the Baptist had not broken this silence; in the account of his preaching that has come to us in the New Testament, John preached in his own name and did not claim to be passing on a "word of God" like the older prophets. But now the word

15

that is heard over Jesus comes from the heavens, from the cosmic dwelling place of God. Located at the start of his public ministry in Galilee,[6] the baptismal theophany places this first part of Jesus' ministry under the light of the unique relationship of Jesus to God in heaven - the Father, his Father - and to the divine Spirit. Placed by Matthew between two prophecies of the passion, by Mark and Luke just after a prophecy concerning the Son of Man and a promise about the kingdom of God soon to come with power, the transfiguration places the journey to Jerusalem and the passion under the same light. Even the death on the cross, this most unexpected and perplexing conclusion of Jesus's ministry, manifests the glory which Jesus has with his Father and with the divine Spirit. Obviously, such a point could not be made before the disciples perceived the renewed presence and power of Jesus after his death and burial. The rising of Jesus justified and transformed the memory of his earlier life. For what he now was in the eyes of the disciples, Jesus must have been all along, even when his followers, blinded, did not understand the import of the events they were living. Jesus is the beloved Son of the eternal Father.

But there was no intrinsic reason why such a conviction would include in this unique relationship to God only the adult, public life of Jesus. Whatever Mark may have thought of this, Matthew and Luke felt it important to show that Jesus was the beloved Son even before he emerged from the crowds flocking toward Jordan to share John's baptism of penance. In his infancy, at his birth, before his birth, Jesus already was the well-beloved. Only such a conviction could justify the casting of the early life of Jesus into the mythical mold of the infancy narratives.[7] But the modern debate about the historicity of these chapters has closed the eyes of many to their real import. As witnessing to the disciples' final understanding of Jesus the Christ, they belong to the heart of the kerygma and they constitute an integral element of the Christian experience. If

16

the old Law called for a relationship to God in-
volving the whole heart, the whole soul and the
whole strength (Deut. 6:5), and this on the part
of every member of Israel, all the more reason to
trust that Jesus belonged totally to God, not only
in his public words and deeds, but also before, in
all aspects and moments of his existence. If the
prophet Samuel could have been offered to the Lord
in his infancy, Jesus must have been with the Lord
even before his infancy: he was not offered to
God by his parents; he came from God to his parents. His conception and his birth themselves
present a Trinitarian character: it is by the
power of the divine Spirit that Jesus is conceived
by his mother, in keeping with the plan of God
symbolically communicated to Mary by the archangel
Gabriel.[8]

The next step in the assertion of the divine
dimension of Jesus's life from its beginning is
taken in the Johannine gospel. There is no need,
here, for a mythical presentation of the birth and
infancy of Jesus, for this is preempted by the
doctrine of the first chapter: Jesus is the Logos
become flesh. And the Logos - the Dabar of Judaism, the Wisdom (Hochma, Sophia) of the Old Testament - is with God and is God. The message that
"the Logos became flesh" (J., 1:14) implies the
unstated anti-docetic requirement that, from his
becoming flesh on, the Logos always remains flesh.
Were he to cease being flesh, he would not be
Logos anymore. And just as the Logos of God is
visible in the flesh, so is his flesh transformed
by the Logos. The resurrection is implicit from
the very first lines of the Johannine gospel. And
the Johannine account of the post-Easter appearances is in line with this: Jesus does not want to
be touched by Mary (20:17). He is flesh enough to
be touched: he shows his hands and his side to the
disciples and to Thomas (20:20 and 27). But this
is no longer the time to be touched; now is the
time for the full revelation of what he is, as
Logos, in relation to his Father. He has to go to
the Father (20:17). His going will reveal the
sense of his rising from the dead. The Logos can-

17

not be contained by she'ol because "in him was life" (1:4). He cannot be bound by the limitations of this world because he is "from the beginning", and he is with "the God, and he is God" (1:1).

In the light of this Johannine emphasis, the famous passage of 8:58 acquires its full meaning: "Before Abraham was, I am." At this moment Jesus makes a statement about his pre-existing to Abraham, in answer to a direct challenge from the Pharisees: "You are not yet fifty. How can you have seen Abraham?" (8:57) Taken literally, this would only be a paradoxical saying, for which Jesus could be considered crazy, but which would not deserve stoning. If his challengers want to stone him (v. 59), this is because they have perceived the sharp edge of his answer. Jesus has pronounced the divine name, I am, under whose aegis Moses was sent to the people: "This is what you shall tell the Israelites: I am sent me to you" (Ex. 3:14). This name is the heart of the revelation of the Exodus. It is normative and paradigmatic for all subsequent revelation. In John's theology, therefore, Jesus ties his mission to the original sending of Moses by doing something which no Jew, however holy, would have dreamt of doing: he identifies himself with the sacred name. Jesus is I am, now present in the flesh.

o o o

The book of the New Testament which comes nearest to expressing a fully Trinitarian faith is undoubtedly the Apocalypse. In my judgement, this book originated in Johannine circles, but its author cannot be identified with the author of the gospel and the epistles. I would tend to ascribe the book to John the presbyter, mentioned by Papias. This John the presbyter had considerable importance in the province of Asia toward the end of the first century. The tradition of Polycarp and Irenaeus apparently derives from him. He in turn seems to have been a disciple of the author of the Johannine gospel.[9]

Be that as it may, the book of Revelation is written under a predominant Trinitarian image, which recurs principally in 1:4-6; 1:13-20; 4:2-5, and which is alluded to throughout the book. This image is presented progressively. It should be seen as an apocalyptic transformation of the gospel images of the Three, which we have found in the accounts of the baptism and of the transfiguration.

A first allusion to the threefoldness of God introduces the messages to the seven churches of Asia, or, more accurately, to the totality of all the churches, symbolized by the perfect number 7: "Grace and peace, from him who is and was and is to come, and from the seven spirits before his throne, and from Jesus Christ, the faithful witness, the first-born from the dead and ruler of the kings of earth" (1:4-5). The expression, "him who is and was and is to come" elaborates for non-Jewish readers what was conveyed by the sinaitic revelation of the divine name, I am, and by its reinterpretation in the I am of the Johannine gospel. As such, it is not directly Trinitarian. The text does not refer to God the Father, but to Jesus Christ who is I am. The present participle, used here, (literally, "the being") is borrowed from the Septuagint Greek rendering of the Hebrew form. And since Jesus is I am, one must also, looking back upon the past history of revelation, say that he was. One may wonder if this 'was' should not be understood with the aorist rather than the imperfect meaning: he was and continues to be into the present, although this would not make any difference from a theological point of view.[10] That the writer, changing verbs, switched next to the future participle of the verb, to come, is not without significance. The point is not that he will be, since the one who is, understood in the perspective of the Old Testament name, I am what I am (Ex. 3:14), will ever be. The author refers rather to the future coming, to what Pauline literature calls the parousia. Seven spirits stand before the throne. The throne should be read as a symbol of the Divinity, in keeping with the merkabah mysticism of Jewish tradition. The seven spirits I identify, not directly with the Spirit of God, but with the "angels of the presence" who, in patristic literature, stand nearest to the throne of God.[11] The separate mention of "Jesus Christ the faithful witness, the first-born from the dead and ruler of the kings of earth" does not imply that it is the Father who sits on the divine throne. In the perspective of the Apocalypse, one and the same person "is, was, and is to come", and sits on the throne: it is Jesus Christ the faithful witness. This is quite clear in verse 8: "The Lord God says: I am the alpha and the omega, the one who is and who was and who is to come, the almighty". Belonging to the realm of language, the terms, alpha and omega, cannot qualify any other than the one whom the gospel of John calls the Logos. Alpha and omega pertain to the Word. Being the first and the last letter both of the alphabet and of the vowel system, they indicate the sum-total of all that God says. The phrase does not quite equate the other expressions, "I am the first and the last" (1:17 and in 22:13), or "the beginning and the end" (22:13). First and last evoke resurrection and judgment. Beginning and end evoke two aspects of the creative act, genesis and eschaton. Alpha and omega refer to the fulness of the Word, which encompasses all that is between the first and the last letters of the alphabet, all actual and possible combinations of letters. Only the Logos can be alpha and omega, for he is all that is spoken by God.

In this blessing, therefore, the Logos is both Yahweh and Jesus the Lord incarnate. As Yahweh he sits on the divine throne; as Jesus he is the faithful witness on earth and in heaven.

The vision which opens the address to the seven churches (1:12-18) confirms this perspective. John sees the Son of Man, of Daniel 7:13, dressed with all the characteristics of the eschatological judge. The Son of Man identifies himself with Jesus, who is "the first and the last, the living one", who "was dead", but now is "living for ever

20

and ever." (1:17-18). Further descriptions of the
Son of Man are given, in keeping with the nature
of each of the seven messages. The messages,which
come from Jesus, are presented to the churches by
the Spirit. The Father is explicitly mentioned at
the end of the fourth, fifth, and seventh messages,
and equivalently at the end of the sixth, where
"my Father" is replaced by "my God". In each case,
the pattern is the same: Christ will reward those
who win the victory, making them share in his own
relationship to his Father. The victor will be
given authority, "the same authority I received
from my Father" (Thyatira, 2:26). He "will be
clothed in white", being acknowledged "in the
presence of my Father and his angels" (Sardis,
3:5). To Philadelphia Christ says: "I will make
the victor a pillar in the temple of my God and he
shall never leave it. I will inscribe on him the
name of my God and the name of the city of my God,
the new Jerusalem which he will send down from
heaven, and my own name which is new" (3:12).
Finally, the victor "will have the right to sit
with me on my throne, as I myself won the victory
and took my seat beside my Father on his throne"
(Laodicea, 3:21). There is a progressive closeness to the Father, from authority to presence to
the city to the throne. Thus the letters orient
the reader toward the revelation of the Father.

It is precisely on a vision of the Father that
the great revelation opens in chapter 4. "A throne
was standing there in heaven, and on the throne
was someone seated." This time, in keeping with
the promise made in the messages, the Father sits
on the throne of the Divinity. But, following the
apophatism of the Jewish tradition, John gives no
name to the Father. He describes the One on the
throne with features borrowed from the visions of
Ezechiel and Isaiah, and with an allusion to the
glory (shekinah) which surrounds him. The setting
is liturgical; it derives from descriptions of the
Temple in the Old Testament. Here again, the
"seven spirits of God", the angels of the presence,
stand before the throne. The One on the throne is
"the living one for ever and ever" (4:9 and 10),

the creator (4:11). This time, Jesus appears as "a lamb that had been slain" (5:6). But the lamb is also on the throne; his seven eyes are "the seven spirits of God sent to all parts of the world" (5:6), identical with the seven angels. And the slain lamb, in a supremely ironic imagery, is also "the lion of the tribe of Juda, the root of David" (5:5).

There is no need, at this point, to review the unfolding of the central vision of the Apocalypse. The four septets (the messages, the seals, the trumpets, the cups) correspond to the four angels of 7:1, whose symbolism successively evokes (1) judgment and warning, (2) the triumph of the Lamb, (3) the destruction of the cosmos (8-14), and the eschatological struggle shown in a series of contrasting and interlocking visions (the two faithful martyrs, 11:1-15, the Woman clothed with the sun, 12, the two beasts, 13), (4) the triumph of the Lamb-Son of Man (14), which entails the destruction of the cosmos (15-16) and of the Great Prostitute-Babylon (17-18), the binding of Satan (19:11-20:10), and the destruction of death (20:11-15). This leads to the ultimate revelation of the new heaven and the new earth, which is itself centered on a new triadic vision of God.

The purpose of this final series of visions is made clear by a loud voice coming from the throne: "Here is the dwelling of God with men" (21:3). In fact, we are given a preview of the faithful part of humankind being introduced into the complex of figures on and around the throne. The One on the throne is simultaneously, though not confusedly, the Father and the Son of Man. Only the Son of Man can, as we have seen, say: "I am the alpha and the omega" (21:6). But only the Father can say of the winner: "I shall be his God and he shall be my Son" (21:7), since filiation by any standard makes sense only in relation to fatherhood. The closeness of the Father and the One like a Son of Man is clearly indicated by the fact that both are "the One who sits on the throne." The triadic picture is completed, at this point, by the sug-

22

gestion that a gift is still to come: "To the thirsty I will give of the source of life, freely" (21:6).

What this source of life is appears in the complementary vision which follows. In the descent of the new Jerusalem "from heaven, from God" (21: 10), the city "shines with the very glory of God" (21:11). It shares, or itself is, the divine glory; it is the new setting of the throne of God (22:3). "The Lord, the almighty God with the lamb, is its Temple" (21:22). The city now shares some of the aspects of the One on the throne. The Father and the lamb are no longer contrasted with the faithful witnesses. For, if the faithful witnesses still constitute a worshipping throng around the throne, they now carry the divine name on their forehead (22:4). They are included in the nearness of the Son of Man to his Father, incorporated into the realm of Divinity. This corresponds to the Danielic vision, in which the "people of the saints of the Most High" (Dan. 7:27) are given the same "kingship and dominion and majesty" as the "One like a Son of Man coming on the clouds of heaven" (Dan. 7:13). Here also, what belongs to the One on the throne is extended to the faithful. Furthermore, the vision of the throne of God and of the city climaxes the entire Revelation, with a clearer reference than before to what later Christian theology will call the Holy Spirit. Prepared by frequent allusions throughout the Apocalypse to the guiding and inspiring action of the Spirit, adumbrated in the reference of 21:6 to the source of living water, the explicit vision of 22:1 completes the previous perceptions: "He showed me the river of living water, clear as crystal, which issued from the throne of God and of the Lamb, and flowed down the middle of the streets." The Spirit, flowing from the throne of the Father and of the Son of Man, fills the city which is the church of the saints. Here the scriptural revelation of the Three reaches its zenith. It heralds a progressive discovery of the Three which must reach its acme at the eschaton.

o o o

The interest in the historicity and the humanity of Jesus which has prevailed in the scientific study of the New Testament since the middle of the last century, has had the good effect of drawing attention to the diverse strains of christological thought present in the early Church. Whatever Jesus really thought of himself, he was understood during the first and second generations of his disciples to have fulfilled the different types of messianic or quasi-messianic expectations present in the Judaism of his times. He was Messiah, Prophet, Servant of God, Son of Man, Son of God, Word of God, High Priest of the New Covenant. These views and several others are reflected in the New Testament itself, written by disciples of the second and third generation (if one may put Paul, who had not witnessed the public ministry of Jesus, in the second generation).

This historical concern has also had the unfortunate effect of blinding many readers to the necessary context for any attempt to define Jesus of Nazareth's spiritual identity. This context is the radical newness of the experience of God which Jesus had. The memory of it among his disciples contributed the most fruitful yet the most mysterious element of their world outlook. The authors themselves of the New Testament, and presumably the communities in which they lived and from whose traditions they extracted their information about Jesus, had been as explicit as it was possible to be about this unique aspect of their Lord. They could not conceptualize clearly or uniformly what Jesus himself had only hinted at. Furthermore, their own reflection about this could not, without jeopardising the apologetic edge of their proclamation to the Jews, separate the God of Jesus from the God of the Temple and of the synagogue. Nor could they, without hiding what was most typical of Jesus, identify the Christian cult of God with the Jewish cult. God had not been experienced in the same way by Judaism and by Jesus. Those who experienced the abiding influence of Jesus of

Nazareth risen from the dead and present with them in the Spirit, and who took his experience of God as paradigmatic for their life, could no longer think of God in the same way as the continuing Judaism of the first centuries after Christ.

In these conditions, and in the absence of clear delineations coming from Jesus, the Christians had to choose between three doctrines of God.

The Elohim of the Old Testament and the Jews could be identified with the Father for whom Jesus had used the term Abba, and whom he had also designated as the Father of his own disciples. In this case, Jesus the Christ has a unique relationship to the Father, which is expressed emphatically in the title, Son of God. Then also, the Holy Spirit, who, in keeping with Old Testament language, represents God in the action of guiding selected individuals and communities among those who believe, entertains his own unique relationship to the Father, which is not clearly outlined. On the whole, this would seem to be the general line of thought followed by the synoptic gospels.

Yet Elohim could also be identified with Jesus in the divine dimension recognized in him by the faith of his followers. In this case, the Father of Jesus Christ, the Abba whom Jesus invoked in prayer, is somehow further removed into divine transcendence. From him "the mystery" emerges in revelation; he is the invisible origin of the Christ and, in another sense, of all things. It is, however, this Elohim, who stands at the source of the divine initiative on earth. In the Old Testament Elohim speaks through the prophets. In the New he is incarnate as Jesus of Nazareth, who is shown by his resurrection to be the Lord, the Adonai of the Old Testament. Then the divine Spirit, who also guides the faithful on earth, is the Spirit of our Lord Jesus Christ; it is the Lord at work after his Lordship has been proclaimed. By and large, this corresponds to the theology of Paul, who may have been the first to apply the concept of Lordship to this divine dimension

25

of Christ as Elohim. It is also the theology of the Johannine writings, where the concept of Logos plays a similar role.

Elohim, however, could also conceivably be identified with the whole divine sphere represented by the baptismal formula, "the Name of the Father, the Son, and the Holy Spirit" (Matt. 28: 19). This is not clearly present anywhere in the New Testament. Yet it seems to be suggested by some of the expressions used in the pastoral epistles. Here, "God the Father" and "Christ Jesus our Lord" (2 Tim. 1:1) are distinguished. Yet both are "our savior" (Tit. 3:4-6), and Jesus himself is "our great God and savior" (Tit. 2:13). No doubt, such a vocabulary was influenced by the redemptive context of the religions of salvation which, in the form of mystery-cults, were then spreading in the hellenistic world. The chief characteristic of God in relation to humankind is to be savior. Presumably the application of the title of Savior equivalently to Christ and to God in the deutero-Pauline letters brings about a similar use of the name, God, applied now both to God and to Jesus Christ. Were this extended to the Spirit – as will be done in later Christian literature – the three, Father, Son and Spirit, would be jointly Elohim.

The first line of thought, typical of Judeo-Christian theology, survived until the waning of Judeo-Christianity before the end of the second century. The second, which is more emancipated from the Old Testament and the semitic matrix, became particularly well developed among the Greek Fathers of the Church. The third strand of thought presupposes a more philosophical reflection about the divine nature and the Three whom Christians experience as one God: this anticipates a later and more Western development, illustrated especially in the works of St. Augustine.

The developed doctrine of the Trinity was progressively formulated through the ecumenical councils of Nicaea (325), Constantinople I (381), Constantinople II (553) and III (680-81), and through

26

a number of regional councils, among which the councils of Toledo have particular importance. It was refined through the reflection of the great Fathers, especially St. Basil and St. Gregory Nazianzen in the East, with Tertullian and St. Augustine in the West. But the New Testament was and remains the exact locus of the revelation of the doctrine. This doctrine did not come fully formulated and explained. Yet it was fully revealed to the disciples in their experience of Jesus. Jesus the Christ, who died and rose from the dead in the power of the divine Spirit, must be called the revealer of the Father who sent him, of the Son who he himself is, of the Spirit in whom he rose and whom he left to the disciples as their Consoler.

1. On the importance of this name for God, see Joachim Jeremias: The Prayers of Jesus, Philadelphia, 1978.

2. On Jewish mysticism see Gershom Scholem: Major Trends in Jewish Mysticism, Jerusalem, 1941; Kabbalah, Jerusalem, 1974.

3. Martin Luther: The Freedom of a Christian Man, 1521, in John Dillenberger: Martin Luther, Selections from his Writings, New York, 1961, p. 53.

4. On messianic expectation in the Old Testament, see S. Mowinckel: He That Cometh, Oxford, 1951.

5. The two expressions would be identical in Hebrew, since Elohim, the common word for God, literally means, the heavens.

6. Mk 1:9-11; Mt 3:13-17; Lk 3:21-22; J 1:29-34.

7. Here and elsewhere in this book I use the words, myth, mythical, in their modern sense as defined in structural anthropology; see Claude Lévi-Strauss: Anthropologie structurale. Deux, Paris, 1973, p. 139-315.

8. Lk 1:26-39. I do not take sides here on the question of the historicity of the Annunciation. But whatever the facts, the Annunciation and belief in Mary's virginal maternity (which I take to be implied in Luke's story) make a major christological point: the conception and birth of the Savior are as exclusively due to the divine initiative as salvation through the Savior is by grace alone, not by the works of the Law or the works of human nature. The later doctrine of Mary's permanent virginity is a proper assumption if divine grace is conceived as establishing a permanent relationship, and not only as enabling Mary to assent to a passing act of God. How could the one who agreed to be transformed by the divine initiative leading to the birth of the Messiah, later yield to the sexual initiatives of a man? See the debate in Raymond Brown: The Virginal Conception and Bodily

Resurrection of Jesus, New York, 1973; The Birth of the Messiah, Garden City, N.J., 1977; R. Brown et al.: Mary in the New Testament, New York, 1978.

9. See the discussion of Johannine authorship in Brown: The Gospel according to John, vol.I, Garden City, N.J., 1966, p. lxxxvii-civ.

10. The switch, in the formula, "who is, who was, who is to come" (Rev., 1:4), from the present participle of to be, to the third person singular of the imperfect of to be, and to the future participle of to come, is grammatically odd. It seems clear that the writer could not find a regular grammatical form expressing what the second term was meant to convey. This applies also if the formula was borrowed from some liturgical usage.

11. See Tavard: Die Engel, Freiburg, 1968, p.20-21; 31-32. The number of these "protoctist" (first-created) angels is usually given by the Church Fathers as six, the number seven, when used, including most often Christ as the Angel of the Great Counsel.

II

The Vision

Several Roman sarcophagi, presumably dating
from the fourth century, represent the Trinity in
bas-relief. The very presence of such sculpture
in the art of the early Church suggests interesting questions. Why should any one, at that time -
or, for that matter, more recently - wish to have
the Trinity represented on a coffin, or, to trans-
pose this in the contemporary setting, on a funeral monument? Funeral art is, at all periods,
conservative. It does not aim at giving people an
existential shock, at pushing them toward new
awareness of self or toward a breakthrough in the
investigation of the mystery of life. People put
on their tombstones or, in ancient Roman civilization, on their sarcophagi, pictures of what is
dear to them. Familiar objects and symbols are
most proper. When friends visit the cemetery for
a refrigerium (the commemorative meal of Roman
custom), or on All Souls' day as it developed in
the Middle Ages under the influence of Cluny, they
are reminded of the dead who are buried at this
spot by seeing symbols and pictures that were
meaningful to them. Not infrequently, a sarcophagus will show the face of the couple buried in
it, united in death as in life. Presumably,there-
fore, the biblical and the Christian scenes of the
sarcophagi were chosen because of their familiar
meaning. Whether a rich person ordered a sarcophagus and specified what was to be shown upon its
sides, or a less well-to-do citizen selected a
ready-made one, the choice must have been guided
by the importance, the meaning and the familiarity
of its art.

The Christian art of the cemeteries of the
first centuries systematically features the themes
of hope and resurrection. It is an art of comfort
and consolation by which the trials of this world,
particularly acute in periods of persecution, are
counterbalanced by a clear afffirmation of the
resurrection.

Facing death, salvation, redemption, or justification imply resurrection. If these can be given other connotations as regards Christian life here below, it is the hope of resurrection which predominates as soon as one is concerned with death and dying. The fate of the Christian dead is symbolized by the image of the orant raising his hands to God in prayer and thanksgiving. In such a context, the simple fact that the Trinity may be depicted shows that the Trinity must have evoked, with the creation of life at the hands of the divine Word, and its re-creation through baptism and faith, the renewal of life beyond death.

Two of these sarcophagi, closely related in style and motifs, must have originated in the same workshop, in spite of the distance between the places where they have been found. One is at the Vatican Museum in Rome.[1] The other, discovered only in 1974, is now displayed in the Musée Chrétien of Arles in France.[2] They are very similar in design: two rows of scenes, the upper one being interrupted by a medallion with the portrait of a defunct couple. We will concentrate on the extreme right of the sarcophagi. In the one that I shall call sarcophagus I, the upper level shows the Three Persons in the form of three bearded men wearing the philosopher's mantle. The first is standing, his right hand holding the back of the chair on which the second is sitting. The second sits, his feet on a stool, his right hand extended in a gesture of blessing and touching the third man's right arm, his left hand resting in his lap. The third is standing, his face turned right toward the first two, who are both looking in his direction, his right hand resting on the head of Eve, his left hand not being visible. Eve, who is, like Adam, of the size of a child, is standing, having just emerged from Adam who is still asleep on the ground.[3]

In sarcophagus II, the first two men are practically the same as in sarcophagus I. Part of the arm of the second is broken, but the hand remains, touching the arm of the third in a gesture of

blessing. The third is beardless; his left hand
holds a scroll, and his right rests on the head of
Eve, who is now standing next to Adam at her left
side.

The scene at the lower level in both sarcophagi is that of the Epiphany. Mary sits on a
throne, her feet on a stool, and holding the child
in her lap. Behind her there stands a man who
looks exactly the same as the one behind the
throne of the upper level. The child is receiving
the gift of the first of the magi, whose hand
points to the star above.

In both cases the scenes of the creation of
Eve and of the epiphany closely correspond. It is
as though the artist had intended to suggest a
close parallelism between what we may call the
Three in heaven and the Three on earth. The
Spirit, the Father, the Son overshadow the Spirit,
the Mother, the Son. For the person who stands
behind Mary's throne, whose features are perfectly
identical with those of the first man above, has
to be identified with the Holy Spirit. It is the
Spirit, whose "overshadowing" the Virgin is an-
nounced by the archangel Gabriel (Lk. 1:35), and
of whom Matthew says that Mary "found herself preg-
nant from the Holy Spirit" (Mt 1:18). In the scene
at the upper level, therefore, the first man is
the Spirit; the Father is seated on the throne;
the Son or Logos comes next. In sarcophagus I,
the Logos is shown in his divinity, sharing the
same philosophical features, notably the beard, as
the other two. In sarcophagus II, the Son is
beardless, this being the convention in early
church art: after the fashion of Roman aristo-
cracy,Jesus is given the attributes of the Kyrios,
the Emperor of the universe.[4] Here too Jesus
holds a scroll in his left hand, either the gospel
or the book of life. It goes without saying that
the Jesus thus shown is not presented only in his
humanity; he is the Christ of Colossians 1:15-18,
"the first-born of all creatures, for it is in him
that all things have been created."

This is a creation scene. The creative power originates in the One on the throne, from whose right shoulder the gesture of creation is transmitted to the arm of the Son extended for blessing. The Spirit, standing in the background, overshadows the scene, looking benevolently upon it as he looks benevolently on the magi's visit to the child. Clearly, sarcophagus I depicts the scene of Genesis 2:21-22. The creating hand of the Logos rests on Eve's head as she has just emerged from Adam at the Logos's bidding. Adam is still absorbed in his mystical sleep. Adam and Eve have the stature of children, in keeping with the theology of St. Irenaeus. As I have shown elsewhere, the emergence of Eve constitutes the acme of the creative process.[5] This gives special poignancy to the attitude of the Spirit, who surveys the scene from behind the Father's throne. There is a trace of a smile on his face, as on the Father's. While he is, as it were, hidden behind the throne, he also looks like a prompter with a special stake in what is happening. This is especially clear in sarcophagus II, where he not only holds the Father's throne, but is also slightly bent toward the Father's shoulder where the creating movement starts. He is not a mere on-looker, but seems to take part in the action by speaking into the Father's ear.

In this second sarcophagus, the scene is not that of Genesis 2. What is depicted is the first story of creation. Adam and Eve, still as children, stand side by side, Eve on Adam's right side. This is in keeping with Roman custom: in the portraits of husband and wife at the center of the sarcophagus the woman is always on the right of the man. The Logos-Jesus still holds his hand on Eve's head. What we see is Genesis 1:37 cast in stone: "God created man in his image; in God's image he created him; man and woman he created them." Adam seems to be presented to God by a man who touches him slightly with his left hand. From his face one can identify St. Paul, with the receding forehead which is commonly given to him in early Christian art. For Paul is the only author in the New Testament who contrasts the first Adam with Christ, the second Adam (Rom. 5).

These creation scenes may have also a further dimension. The first creation is a type of the second; the old creature heralds, and makes place for, the new creature in which it is, for St. Irenaeus, who took his cue from St. Paul, "recapitulated".[6] Thus, Eve is not only the mother of all who live in the flesh; she is also the ecclesia, mother of all who live in the Spirit. Adam is the symbol of Christ, Eve of the ecclesia. In sarcophagus I, Adam's mystical sleep represents the falling asleep of Christ in death, which gave substance and nurture to the ecclesia which emerged from his dying: the ecclesia is thus closely related to the resurrection. In sarcophagus II, Adam relates to the Word, and Eve likewise to the Spirit.

The creation scenes on these sarcophagi imply a statement about God as Triune. When these works of art were being sculptured, the council of Nicaea (325) had taken place. It had affirmed that the Word is homoousios with the Father. But this doctrine, although endorsed originally by Emperor Constantine, recognized by the bishop of Rome and by the main episcopal sees of the East, is not yet fully accepted everywhere. Constantine, impressed by the continuing strength of Arianism, has had second thoughts about the matter. After his death in 337, his son Constantius tried to reverse the position by rejecting the Nicaean dogma and imposing Arianism on the church.[7] In Rome itself, one major work on the Three Persons had already been written: the De Trinitate of Novatianus in the third century.[8] It is interesting to notice some common features in our sarcophagi and in Novatianus's essay. The primordiality of the Father, what authors of the third century had called the "monarchy", is emphasized. Novatianus devotes the first eight of his thirty chapters to a description of the divine nature and attributes, identified precisely with the first Person. In the sarcophagi, the monarchy is indicated by the Father's throne: the Father is the one who presides over all in the attitude of magisterial authority. Novatianus insists on the distinction between the Father and his Son, which is well indicated by the sculpture of the Trinity in the form of three men.

The danger of tritheism which is inherent in this symbolization is happily counterbalanced by the stress on the monarchy. There is of course no attempt, on the part of the craftsmen, to suggest the intra-Trinitarian processions, which can hardly be indicated pictorially. Nor is there any such attempt in Novatianus, who is satisfied with affirming them and asserting, in the line of the theology of Irenaeus, that only the Son knows "the secrets of this sacred and divine nativity."[9] Yet, although the Father is primarily the Creator, the creation is effected through the Son, a point which is well formulated by the writers and equally well shown by the artists. As to the Spirit, Novatianus eloquently affirms his divinity. The only perfect recipient of the Spirit is the Son himself: the Spirit "dwells full and complete in the Son alone." It is from the Son, in whom "the source of the whole holy Spirit remains," that men receive the Spirit, who illumines the prophets, teaches the apostles, enlightens the teachers, leads the faithful, guides the church. It is therefore no surprise that, on the sarcophagi, the Spirit is not in direct contact with the creatures: only through the extended hand of Christ touching Eve is the Spirit's influx channelled down to us. And I sense that, in the epiphany scene, the Spirit standing behind Mary's throne while she holds the child who receives the magi's gifts, also suggests the totality of his presence precisely where Jesus is.

The theological debate about the divinity of the Spirit has not yet generally begun when these sarcophagi are handcrafted. Thus a new dimension of their art is manifest. Theologians like Novatianus have clearly taught the full divinity of the Spirit. But this theology has been implicitly

challenged, in the first quarter of the fourth
century, by Arius. Denying explicitly the full
divinity of the Logos, Arius implicity denied the
divinity of the Third Person. The council of
Nicaea has affirmed the divinity of the Logos by
introducing into the creed the homoousia between
the Father and the Son. In the shifting grounds
of the ensuing controversy the divinity of the
Spirit will be explicitly denied by those who will
be called pneumatomachoi (spirit-killers) by the
orthodox. The Council of Constantinople, in 381,
will include the divinity of the Spirit in the
creed by stating that the Spirit is "lord", that
he proceeds from the Father, and that with the
Father and the Son he is co-adored and con-glorified. The sarcophagi, however, suggest simply
that popular theology in Rome toward the middle
of the century has anticipated the conciliar decision. Unhampered by the theological debates on
homoousios, it has followed the logic of the older
theology formulated by Novatianus.

This might appear more clearly still if the
picture of the Three Persons on a third sarcophagus were well preserved. Unfortunately, what I
will call sarcophagus III has been badly damaged.[10] Here, the Three Persons appear also at the
upper right. There are no immediately connected
other scenes, since this is a "strigyllated" sarcophagus: the scenes are in the form of vignettes
at the four corners, plus a central scene in which
the couple for whom the coffin was made is featured
with Christ, with an allegorical scene underneath.
The Three Persons are standing. Two are in front,
their toga well preserved, but their head gone.
The one on the left I take to be Christ, for his
left hand holds a scroll which his right hand also
seems to touch. The one on the right I identify
as the Father; his right hand is gone, though it
seems to have been blessing Eve, and his left is
extended toward Eve. The central figure, hidden
behind the other two, except for its unbearded
head turned toward the Father, must be the Spirit.
Eve and Adam, as children, are in front of the
Second person, Eve standing and Adam in the pro-

cess of getting up from sleep. The homoousia between the First and the Second Person is suggested by their identical stance in the picture. The Spirit, invisible but for his head, remains somewhat undefined. Yet his lack of a beard shows him to be the Spirit of the Son, for the Son is normally beardless. Together with the Son, the Spirit faces the Father. In sarcophagi I and II, the Spirit and the Father constitute one oriented unit looking toward the Son and Eve, and the Son in turn looks toward them. In sarcophagus III, the directions are reversed: the Spirit and the Son constitute one oriented unit (or we may presume they do, despite the damaged state of the sculpture) looking toward the Father. Is it by sheer coincidence that, shortly after the mid-years of the century, Marius Victorinus, himself a Roman rhetor, elaborated a dyadic theology of the Trinity in which the Second and the Third Persons are collated in front of the Father as together constituting "the Son"? For Victorinus the Spirit is included in the generation of the Son, hidden in him; and it is through the Spirit as eternal Wisdom that the movement from the Father returns to its source. This has a metaphysical basis in the distinction between being (the Father) and form or movement, and in the distinction of two kinds of movement, life (the Word) and thought or wisdom (the Spirit).[11] The craftsman of sarcophagus III is presumably not a metaphysician; yet he has also shown the Spirit emerging from behind Christ, unbearded like Christ, and totally focused on the Father.

All in all, these sarcophagi allow us to draw several conclusions.

Firstly, in Rome in the fourth century, Trinitarian thought pertained to the consoling, salvific truths familiar enough to the people to inspire themes for cemeterial art.

Secondly, the Trinitarian conception of God must have also belonged to the ordinary catechesis in use in the city. And as one of these sarcophagi was found as far as Arles in Southern Gaul, such a catechesis must have been widespread in the Roman sphere of influence.

Thirdly, the understanding of the Trinity did not only take the shape of a doctrine. It was also communicated in the form of a vision, of an image, which artists attempted to reproduce and interpret. It had an esthetic dimension. In the long run, this has far-reaching implications. For a vision is a means of contemplation. Faith related to vision is not only or chiefly obedience to a divine mandate. It is also and primarily joy; it expresses a sense of thanksgiving and awe before the revelation of beauty; it is a matter, no doubt, of assent, but also of imagination.

Fourthly, this esthetic contemplation of the Three follows no set, unalterable pattern. Several models - we have seen three, but there were more - were compatible with the common catechesis. One may discern similarities, if not links, between known theological orientations and the representations of the Trinity. Esthetic pluralism points to some degree of theological pluralism. In the light of the art, it would be trivial and superficial to identify the Roman faith in the Trinity with a subordinatianist or even a cosmological doctrine, even if such may be found in the writings of some theologians.

Fifthly, assent to the doctrine of the Trinity as depicted on our sarcophagi is not in essence intellectual, although it has a noetic aspect. It involves the whole person. For the whole person is called to pass through the shadows of death, and to perceive the comforting vistas of the beyond in the resurrection. The whole person is grasped by the vision of beauty.

Sixthly, the image of the Three in heaven is tied to the image of the two in creation, Eve and Adam. Yet this need not be seen as a cosmological conception of the origin of the Word and the Spirit. Through the vision of Eve emerging from

39

Adam, the artist sees the creation of humankind through the Word. He sees humankind in its two-fold aspect at the moment of the emergence of the church, as Eve, from humanity, as Adam. He sees also the ecclesia emerging from the second Adam. Whence the theological meaning of the childhood of the human figures: it is as children of the Father that, Christian and human, believing and living, in the stance of faith and the dormancy of nature, we receive the revelation of the Three and we contemplate, through Jesus Christ the Son, the monarchy of the Father in the aura of the Holy Spirit.

o o o

Let us now turn to a series of Trinitarian miniatures, painted around 1440 in the Netherlands. The Book of Hours of Catherine of Cleves was illustrated by an unknown artist working in Utrecht. It marks the high point of Dutch illumination and compares well, in its own style, with what was then painted in Paris, the other great center of manuscript decoration. I wish to study a series of illuminations of the Trinity, featured respectively (I) on folio 77v, (II) on 82, (III) on 83v, (IV) on 85, (V) on 86v, (VI) on 88, (VII) on 90.[12] This constitutes a continuous series, which is hardly interrupted by two paintings, God the Father on a throne, on 78, and God the Son on a throne, on 80v. The location of this series in the manuscript is worth noting. The manuscript begins with illustrations of the hours of the Virgin, including a series on her life, from the annunciation to Joachim to the assumption. Then a series on the passion of Christ, ending with the resurrection, illustrates the hours of the Cross. The series on the Trinity follows, illustrating the hours of the Trinity, to be prayed on Sunday. It is followed by the hours and the mass of the dead (Monday), the hours and the mass of the Holy Spirit (Tuesday), the hours and the mass of All Saints (Wednesday), the hours and the mass of the Eucharist (Thursday), the hours and the mass of

40

the Compassion (Friday), the hours and the mass of the Virgin Mary (Saturday). The remaining illuminations illustrate the penitential psalms, the office of the dead, and the feasts of a number of saints.

The Trinitarian miniatures follow two basic styles: the Three Persons on one throne (I, II, III, VI), and the "throne of grace" (V). VII is a variant of the throne of grace. IV, as we will see, follows another style. The theme is dominated by the first of these illuminations. Here, the Three Persons are enthroned in the sanctuary of a gothic church, at the spot where one would expect to find the altar. They go from right to left in the standard order, the Son being in the middle. The Father wears a papal tiara, while the Spirit is dressed in a white alb with a crossed stole like that of a priest, the Son alone having no recognizable clerical garment. The Father is dressed in blue with a purple cope, the Son in purple with a red cope. Each has a halo; the rays of the cross are inscribed in that of the Son; and a dove is perched on that of the Spirit. The Father's right hand rests on a globe supported by his knee; the Son's right hand is extended for blessing, while his left rests on a book, which the Spirit also holds with his left hand. The Father's left hand, the Spirit's right are hidden behind the Son. Several details enhance the prestigious figure of the Son: he alone is in full view, the other two being partly hidden behind him; he alone, looking straight ahead, relates directly to the on-looker; he alone does the gesture of blessing. The Father, having a long white beard, is patterned on "the ancient of days" of the prophet Daniel; his face reflects benevolence and wisdom. The Son, uncrowned and with a small beard, has a majestic face reminiscent of a Byzantine Pantocrator. He is clearly the judge. Whether the book he holds is the book of life or the bible, it functions here as the book of law according to which judgement will be passed. The Spirit's portraiture is the most elusive; his priestly garments seem unusual and theologically puzzling; by his

41

face, he looks like the Son's twin brother, although he is seen at an angle, and his lighter hair, more reddish than brown, gives him a younger and slimmer figure.

This striking image is completed by the miniatures of folio 78 and 89v. In the first, the Father sits alone on a throne, with the same features as before, his left hand on the globe, his right hand raised in blessing, surrounded by a starry blue sky and red clouds in which two angels are flying. The second shows the Son in the same position, dressed as before, his left hand on the book, his right hand raised in blessing, on a black backdrop in which a golden filigree uncoils from behind the throne. Clearly, these two miniatures affirm the equality of the Two in power and glory. As we pass on to (II) the Two are resorbed into the Trinity. Here, the Three on a throne surrounded by a starry blue sky look exactly as in (I), except for the Spirit, with no dove on his halo, and with a book in his right hand, his left being open in a gesture of wonder and admiration. Nine angels of various colors appear at the edge of the picture, five on the Father's side, four on the Spirit's: these are the nine choirs of the angelological tradition. Largely illegible inscriptions near each halo contain the words, Adam, and mors (death), thus suggesting that the Three Persons are weighing the consequences of sin.

There can be no doubt that the painter intended his miniatures of the Trinity to form a meaningful theological sequence. After the Trinity in eternal glory among the angelic choirs (I), he showed the Father and the Son in the act of creation: the Father, with the first hints of the present world in the margin, in the form of grapes and a goat (Ia); then the Son with the first hints of humankind in the margin in the form of a small nude man coming out of a flower armed with bow and arrow (Ib). When we reach (II), Adam has sinned; the face of the Son, majestic in (I), serene in (Ib), now looks reflective and sad. In (III), the process of redemption has been decided. In the margin, humankind works at its chores: a woman plucks a goose and a monkey (!) prepares some kind of potion. Only the First and the Third sit on the throne; the Son, in the middle, kneeling before the Father, receives a cross from the Father's right hand and a blessing from his left; the Spirit encourages the Son, touching him gently on the shoulder. The backdrop is red with golden filigree.

The tone changes with the style of IV, a style which is often found in the iconography of the annunciation and of the baptism by John: the Father appears from the clouds; the Son is on earth, in the river Jordan or near the ear of the Virgin or already within her; the Spirit is symbolized by a dove. This pattern, related to the scriptural accounts of the baptism and of the transfiguration, has been adopted here in reference to redemptive incarnation: the Father appears within red clouds from which rays emerge in the direction of the earth; the Spirit, a dove with a halo and surrounded by flames, is literally diving toward the earth; at the extreme end of this descending movement, the Son, a naked baby, also dives down, head first, holding on to a cross whose bottom is about to touch earth. The sky passes from dark blue at the top to white in the valley where the landing is about to take place. The landscape is of green and slightly brown hills with a tree and some brush or weeds. In the margin, humankind goes on with its works: a fisherman catches fish from a pond.

The throne of grace (V) features at the same time the Trinity and the crucifixion: Jesus is nailed to a cross planted in the globe, now resting on the same tesselated black and yellow floor as in (I). Jesus has died: his side has been pierced by the lance. But the crucifixion is not on a hill outside Jerusalem: it is in the hands of the Father who, seated on a black throne, holds the horizontal beam of the cross, as though holding the orb of the world through the cross, which effectively mediates between him and the world.

The Spirit is in the form of a dove perched on Jesus's halo. The background is red with golden filigree stemming from behind the throne. In the bottom margin, humankind, represented by the two spies sent by Moses into Canaan (Numbers 13), already reaps the fruits of salvation: the spies bring back a sample of gigantic grapes from the promised land.

With miniature (VI) the Three are back on their common throne, dressed as before and in the same position as in (I) but for the Son. His garments are now those of the resurrection: the shroud of the sepulchre covers his loins, the Father holding it as it falls down to the floor; the book has been replaced by the cross, which the Spirit holds with his left hand as it leans against Jesus's left shoulder; the cross stands on top of the globe of the world which is now under Jesus's feet; Jesus is otherwise naked, the marks of the nails being visible, and his right hand touching the wound in his side while his left arm hangs straight down. The margins feature fanciful vegetation, with no allusion to men or animals. The intent is clearly to show the Trinity after the resurrection, when the Word has taken his humanity into heaven and Jesus, seated on the divine throne as the God-man, has been made Lord of the universe. The conclusion is appropriately expressed in miniature (VII): the Three in heaven are worshipped by a variety of men; the Three follow the pattern of the throne of grace, although no throne is visible. The Father, who holds the cross, emerges from within a cloud of red cherubim.

All in all, the vision of the Three has now become the central focus for faith and worship. As Sunday is the high point of the week, the Trinity is the highpoint of all supernatural and natural worlds. Everything relates to the Three. There is no other key to the consistency of the Christian faith in creation and in the incarnation. Only the Trinitarian conception of God allows us to hold together the divine transcendence and the divine immanence, God's sufficiency and God's involvement in creation, in such a way that neither suffers from the other's polarity. Yet the artist has not overcome the difficult tension between equality and hierarchy in the Three. Equality pervades the pictures of the common throne, while hierarchy prevails in the throne of grace and the baptismal style. Do we see the Father as somehow effacing himself behind the Word? This is logical enough, since in final analysis we never perceive the Father, but only the Word, in keeping with John 14:9: "He who sees me sees the Father." As Lord of the universe, the risen Jesus has carried into divine power and glory the humanity that is now the Word's; and we, when admitted to contemplate this vision, are introduced into some degree of sharing this divine power and glory. But insofar as we are thus relating to the divinity of Christ, we must also see something of the Father: the artist does show us the Three. The other styles of the Trinitarian vision are therefore more complete than the common throne, and they better express the process of knowing the Father: it is through the crucified Son that our gaze ascends, by the power of the supporting Spirit, to the fontal source of creation. This can be no other than the fontal source of divinity, whom, inadequately, yet truly, we call the Father. Vision is also participation. We become what we see. If we can see the Three, then we are being incorporated into their mutual relationships.

The peculiar development of Western thought since Augustine is instanced in this series of miniatures. The Three are not contemplated in themselves, but in what they do for us and to us. This movement will culminate in Luther's theology, focused on the pro me of the divine action rather than in the divine action as such. Thus the painter has skillfully incorporated the redemptive incarnation in the life of the Three. The privileged moment for contemplating the Trinity is no longer, as in the fourth century, the moment of creation; it is the moment of redemption. Thus can we also enter the Trinitarian life. By the same token the vision of the Three is subjected to deflections and difficulties that are inherent in trying to understand God in relation to man rather than _in se_.

o o o

This danger surfaces in another representation of the Three, a statue this time, which sums up the profound, yet difficult, yet also comforting teaching that we are not alien to the Trinitarian life. I have found this statue in the parish church of the small town of Bayon, in Lorraine. This is a pieta-like Trinity: the Father has received in his arms the Son who has just been lowered from the cross; the Spirit is a dove on the Son's shoulder. No frills or marginal decorations or colors distract attention. Only the nakedness of white stone faces us. This statue presents a striking feature, which I have not seen so marked in any other work of art: deep sorrow on the Father's face matches suffering on the face of the Son. Even the dove, so often nondescript, seems to be gently resting on the Son, ready to nest in the curve of his neck and shoulder. Everything evokes delicacy and grace. Compassion predominates, the compassion of the Father with the sufferings of the cross, the compassion of our Father with the sorrows of humankind. Redemption is not a complement or a consequence of Trinitarian life; it is the Trinitarian life itself. We see, embodied in stone, all the divine love. For God is love. And when love is compassionate, then God has to be, in a mysterious way, Suffering Love. This Love is totally given: this is what we mean when we speak of the Word as the Beloved, and of the Spirit as the Gift. And it is extended to us, the on-lookers, the adorers, who ask for nothing else than God's love to come alive in us. As we are one with Christ, we receive the Father's Gift. The movement of divine mercy, fully expressed in the Word's incarnation and self-abandonment on the cross, originates in the fontal source of the Word's being, homoousios with the Father, in the ousia, the divine being, which the

46

Word receives from the Father. The passion of the Son entails the compassion of the Father giving divine life in the double act of creation and redemption.

This vision of the Three is both moving and beautiful. Yet it suggests that the Father suffers with the Son with a human father's pain. The traditional pieta attitude of the Mother of Christ truly expresses human piety--pietas connoting originally the parent-child relationship. But it cannot provide a good model for the relation of the First and the Second in God. The Father's compassion is not properly understood by extrapolation from human compassion. For there remains, in the words of Kierkegaard, an "infinite qualitative difference" between God and creation, a difference which scholastic theologians formulated in their doctrine that God is "above all genus." Thus the human vision of the Three should include opposite, if not contradictory, polarities: we cannot relate to God except insofar as God relates to us; and God cannot relate to us as we relate to one another and to God. The divine compassion must be a transpassion.

o o o

I have also sought for the vision of the Three in the admirable icons of the "philoxenia of Abraham". Abraham, in Genesis 18, receives three angels who have taken human form. Under the oaks of Mambre he offers them a meal, and they predict the conception of his son Isaac by Sara. Already the Jewish philosopher-theologian Philo had identified these angels as dimensions of the divine and had even specified that the one who addresses Abraham is a higher angel than the others.[13]

One finds a similar interpretation in some of the icons: Abraham receives the divine Word accompanied by two angels. The angel seated or sometimes standing in the middle is Christ, who dominates the scene by his majesty, who alone has a halo, and who is often the only one of the three doing anything in the picture. But at another

47

stage of reflexion and art the philoxenia of Abraham becomes an image of the hagia trias, the Holy Trinity. The three figures now are equally important, all are involved in the action of the picture. Superficially, this theme is quite simply a conventional, not to say artificial allegory. But it has an unfathomable depth which busy onlookers miss to their own loss. It even presents a great advantage over the western thematisation. The seating of the Three around a table eliminates the conflict between equality and hierarchy. For the sides of the table are equal or, in the frequent case of a round or semi-round table, they have been absorbed into a different pattern. The Three are equally involved in the symbolic meal represented by a dish on the table. Yet differences are expressed in remarkable interplays between the orientation of the three figures, their looks, the curving of the bodies, their gestures, their relations to the other persons in the picture - often Abraham and Sara -, the suggested relations with the open side of the table,directed toward all of us who are contemplating the scene. More than Western illuminations and paintings, the icons of the Three involve a fourth: the on-looker, who cannot fully understand or appreciate the esthetic unless grasped by its religious dimension. I find myself strangely moved by a fresco of the hagia trias in the chapel now called the Karanlik Kilise, at Göreme in Cappadocia:[14] soft tones of blue, red and brown; the curve of eternity enshrining the picture; the eucharistic table in the middle, whose curved shape parallels the greater curve above; the Son, straight ahead of me, quiet and serene, blessing the universe; the Father on his right, bent in a forward-going movement emphasized by the sweep of his wings, the gesture of blessing of his arm, the muscularity of his right leg as though he were about to stand up and run, the slight leaning of the whole body. The face, damaged, no longer evokes any age. Yet this clearly shows the originator, the starter, the runner, the athlete, God in the full possession of immense yet restrained power. Facing him, at the other end of the curved table, I see the Spirit, his head turned and leaning toward the Father, yet his body twisting on itself as though ready to face Sara who stands behind; already shifting position in order to extend his right arm toward her, reaching through Sara to all womankind. As we approach the open side of the table, where curvature gives way to a nearly straight line, we the on-lookers stand between Abraham and Sara, partaking of both, sons and daughters of those who believed and in whom great things happened because of their faith. We approach, and while we believe, we ask the Lord before us to help our unbelief, we wait for the Spirit's hand to touch us gently, for the ineluctable movement initiated in the Father to carry us to the unknown horizons of his will. At this point names are no longer adequate. We speak of the Spirit, but this is the divine Touch embracing us; of the Son, but this is the ocean of divine Serenity supporting us; of the Father, but this is the divine Initiative, the original process, the abyss of loving power from which derive "every good gift, every perfect endowment" (James 1:17), the Light, source of the diffused light of the fresco, in relation to whom the Second is Light-from-Light and the Third is Light-with-Light, and we, the fourth, are reflecting lights in the faith of Sara and Abraham.

The Trinity of Andrei Rublev, undoubtedly the best known of all icons of the philoxenia, evokes another aspect of the Three.[15]   Here Abraham and Sara are not seen; but we may imagine them in front of the picture, at the spot where we are ourselves standing as we look. The background has been reduced to a minimum: the side and roof of a house, a few rocks, and, in the middle, a tree representing the oaks of Mambre. The Three sit somewhat strangely, for one cannot tell if the First and the Third sit on their stools or on the corners of the table. The Logos is in the middle. All the dynamism of the picture is caught in a curving movement from the Spirit by way of the Son to the Father. The artist has shown the Spirit and the Son in their eternal contemplation of the Father; the Father in his eternal inspiration and

49

spiration of the Son and the Spirit. The faces, identical, convey a deep impression of softness and serenity, while the straight position of the First evokes unmeasurable strength, and flexibility appears in the orientation of the Two, drawn as they are to the Origin. A single chalice on the table creates a eucharistic setting which is enhanced by the perception that the peculiar position of the Father and the Spirit carves the white space between them in the shape of a chalice, which enshrines the image of the Son. His face leaning to the Father, the Son carries us with him as we are associated to him through communion; the Spirit also carries us as our eyes follow the bend of his body toward the Son and thence to the Father. In this way the artist brings to its climax the vision of the Three. Only when we are caught in their circular movement of exit and return, their circumincession, can we really see the Three Persons. As long as we remain outside, we look from afar; at best, by faith we see "as in a glass, darkly" (I Cor. 13:12). In order to "know as we are known" (I Cor. 13:13) we have to be inside. Knowledge of the Three is faith as the divine life is proclaimed to us by the Church out of the Scriptures. It becomes theology as we reflect on what the kerygma implies. It has still to be made experience, to be the glance of the mystics, the vision of the initiated, if we are really to know what we believe.

This iconography, it seems to me, has given another solution to the problem faced and inadequately solved by Western art. Since it is by grace that we are saved, we relate to God only in terms of God's relation to us. Yet the divine condescension and compassion - or love - cannot be properly identified as human suffering. Precisely, the icon, by its very structure, leads the eye and imagination beyond the painted surface. The beauty of the image does not function as an end, but as a beginning. It marks the point of departure of an ascent, beyond the image, to the ineffable reality expressing itself through it yet infinitely transcending even the highest creations of the

artistic genius. The statue of the Father's compassion in the church at Bayon leads to a feeling
of both admiration and sorrow in the on-looker, to
an impression of awe before the mystery of the
suffering of God. This may reach deep into one's
soul and elevate one's mind and heart to God, the
Father of the suffering Lord. Yet this is not yet
participation in the relationships of the Three:
the Son is shown dead, helpless, forlorn, abandoned, if not by the Father, yet by life; and the
Spirit's conventional symbol, the dove, hardly
leads us to gauge the depths of the second procession. In contrast, the icon of the philoxenia
of Abraham more successfully leads to a personal
encounter with the Three, beyond what is shown of
their image as conceived by the artist, in God's
very life. With Abraham and Sara, whether shown
or implied, the faith which we share as Christian
believers is directly involved in the Three. We
are visited by God who sits at our table, and the
breaking of the bread opens our eyes, not only, as
at Emmaus, to the authenticity of the risen Jesus,
but also to the fulness of divine life in the
Spirit and the Word, who lead to the inexhaustible
Fountain and Source of all. And once we have been
made to partake of the ineffable exchange between
the Three, we no longer need the device used by a
Western sculptor to show us the divine mercy: the
Father is not like a sorrowful man receiving the
dead body of a crucified Son. We know that the
Source of divinity is infinite love because we now
experience this love. Only in mystical experience
can the full import of Trinitarian doctrine be
perceived.

o o o

"The man looking at the icon directs his mind
to higher contemplation," thus does the byzantine
poet Agathias (c.436-c.582) express the purpose of
the art.[16] Other byzantine authors specify that
a condition for this higher contemplation is
eusebeia, not just piety in the usual sense of the
term, but an attention that is so intent on the
things of God that it discerns the spiritual sense

of the symbolic world where we live. Through the Spirit we perceive hidden dimensions. To those who are endowed with eusebeia the icon opens a window on the divine. By way of the icon of the philoxenia we ourselves welcome the One who is supremely strange and alien to this-worldly concerns. New Abrahams, new Saras, we receive at our table the Three whose totality exhausts the inexhaustible divinity. Although the Fathers of the Second Council of Nicaea (787) did not explicitly advert to the icon of the philoxenia, their general teaching about icons is to the point here: "The one who venerates the icon venerates in it the hypostasis of the one who is depicted".[17]

Western theologians and bishops were much slower than the orientals to acknowledge holy pictures as more than educational and catechetical tools. Shortly after Nicaean Council II, the theologians of Charlemagne at the council of Frankfort of 794 even assailed the Greeks for overrating the veneration that could be extended to pictures. Although they also denounced the iconoclasts, they refused to see that the icon, properly understood, leads to an insight into spiritual realities.[18] Yet it was the doctrine of Nicaea II, and not that of the Libri carolini, which the Council of Trent endorsed at its twenty-fifth session (Dec. 3-4 1563). Against the iconoclasm of the Reformation the Tridentine fathers upheld the ligitimacy of venerating "images of Christ, of the Virgin mother of God, and of the other saints", "not because one believes that there is in them some kind of divinity or power... but because the honor extended to them is refered to the prototypes which they represent, so that through the images which we kiss and before which we uncover and bow our head, we adore Christ and we venerate the saints whose likeness they bear".[19]

One could object that there is no parity between a picture of Jesus Christ and one of the Three Persons. The picture of Jesus shows a man whom one can imagine to be Jesus. But there is no way to represent God, either as One or as Three. This question is examined at length in a little known document of pope Benedict XIV (1740-1758). This was occasioned by a query about the lawfulness of representing the Holy Spirit as a young man. The negative principle is clearly stated: "It would be an impious and sacrilegious error to think that God, the Ultimate Good, the Most High, can be shown in colors as he is in himself."[20] But there is also a positive principle, exactly that which prevails in the oriental icons: "God is represented in the way and the form in which we read in the Holy Scriptures that he condescended to appear to men." "When one reads in the Sacred Letters that God showed himself to human eyes in this or that form, why should it not be licit to paint him in the same form?" "It is not licit to exhibit an image of a divine Person to be seen by human eyes, except in the form in which it is said in the Holy Scriptures that this Person appeared to men at one time." Accordingly, Benedict XIV rejects the image of the Spirit as a young man, but accepts the dove and the pentecostal flames. He rejects the picture of a three-headed man, or of the Virgin carrying the Three in her womb; but he recognizes as lawful the icon of the three who appeared to Abraham, or the throne of grace, where the Father is the "Ancient of days" of Daniel 7:9 associated to an image of Christ and one of the Spirit as a dove. The pope also admits the pieta-like figure of the Ancient of days with the dead body of his Son and the dove, and the picture of the Three as three identical men.

Admittedly, pope Benedict's solution is not completely satisfactory. For it does not explain why the biblical symbolization of the Three, made in the medium of discourse and writing, can be transposed into the other media of painting and sculpture. This type of question requires a more comprehensive theory of symbol than was available in the seventeenth century. Yet, Benedict XIV did express what was the general assumption behind the work of both the Western craftsmen and the icon-painters of Greece and Russia: one cannot invent new symbols of the Three, but one may use the symbols of the biblical tradition.

o o o

I doubt that the position of Benedict XIV has been instrumental in encouraging Christian artists to contemplate the Three. Yet it has successfully ruled out images and pictures that would be gravely misleading. Even if art is not the only or - except perhaps in Orthodox piety - the chief way of divine contemplation, there is a remarkable convergence between what artists have expressed, what the faithful have perceived of divine life, and what the Church's leaders have recognized as proper and lawful in Christian imagination. This convergence confirms the insight of Scripture, that the life of God, before being formulated in doctrine, gives rise to a vision. If indeed we are called to believe, faith does not end when we have recited the baptismal or the Nicene creed and grasped their Trinitarian form. Faith leads us on into the mystery, not as a clear, distinct, particular expression of what God is or does, but as a structured insight, a focussed contemplation, an ordered experience which speaks to the imagination more powerfully, more deeply, than to the intellect. In the darkness of unknowing we know God. In profound obscurity the vision of the Three shines like a timid intimation of dawn, like the promise of a morning knowledge beyond all imagination and description.

1. Reproduced in Giuseppe Wilpert: I Sarcofagi
Cristiani Antichi, Rome, 1929-36, Tavola, vol. I,
tav. LXXXXVI, with commentary in, op. cit., Testo,
vol. II, p. 226.

2. Reproduced in Connaissance des Arts, n. 270,
Paris, August 1974.

3. That Adam and Eve were children before the
fall was part of the theology of St Irenaeus of
Lyon.

4. Beardlessness is a common feature of the iconography of the emperors. Only Marcus Aurelius is
shown with a beard, because he is also a philosopher.

5. Woman in Christian Tradition, Notre Dame, 1973,
p. 25.

6. Ephesians, 1:10; St Irenaeus: Adversus Haeres-
es, III, 21, 10 ff (S. Chr., 211, Paris,1974, p.
426-31).

7. On these developments see Iaroslav Pelikan:
The Emergence of the Catholic Tradition (100-600),
Chicago, 1971, p. 221-277.

8. P. L., 3:911-982.

9. P. L., 3:978. The following quotes are from
972 and 973.

10. Reproduced in Wilpert, op. cit., Tavola, vol.I,
tav. CLVI. This sarcophagus is at the Vatican
Museum, section of paleo-Christian art. There are
other sarcofagi, that I need not study here, which
feature the three Persons: with Abel (Wilpert, op.
cit., Tavola, vol. II, tav. CLXXXI, n. 5); with
Abraham at the scene of the sacrifice of Isaac
(Tavola, vol. II, n. I and 2). See the commentary
in Wilpert, op. cit., Testo, vol. II, p. 230 and
234.

11. See Marius Victorinus: Traités théologiques sur la Trinité (S. Chr., 68, Paris, 1960)..

12. My references are to John Plummer, ed.: The Hours of Catherine of Cleves, New York, n.d.,where the miniatures are reproduced. The original manuscript is in the Piermont Morgan Library in New York City.

13. Philo, vol. VI: De Abrahamo,XXII, p. 107-13 (Loeb Classical Library, Cambridge-London, 1935).

14. See Marcell Restle: Byzantine Wall Painting in Asia Minor, 3 vol., Greenwich, Conn., 1967.

15. Reproduced in Eugene Trubetskoi: Icons: Theology in Color, New York, 1973. The original is at the Tretyakov State Gallery, Moscow.

16. Quoted in Gervase Mathew: Byzantine Aesthetics, New York, 1971, p. 78.

17. Conciliorum Oecumenicorum Decreta, Basle, 1962, p. 112.

18. In fact the Libri Carolini (P.L.,98:1000-1248), where the Carolingian doctrine is formulated,follow and expand principles already expressed by pope Gregory the Great in two letters to the bishop of Marseille: P.L., 77:1027-28; 1128-30. On the controversy, see Iaroslav Pelikan: The Spirit of Eastern Christendom (600-1700), Chicago, 1974, p. 91-145.

19. C. O. D., p. 751; Denzinger-Schönmetzer, n. 1823.

20. Benedicti XIV Bullarium, vol. I, Prato, 1845, p. 573; the following quotes are from p. 573 and 575.

III

The Speculation

The purpose of the present chapter is neither to outline the historical development of Trinitarian doctrine and theology, nor to elaborate a new theological synthesis on the Trinity. It is, more modestly, to reflect on some basic aspects of theological reflection about the Tri-une God. I have indicated in a previous writing that, in a sense, Trinitarian doctrine, though fully unfolded in Christianity, accounts for the entire gamut of world religions.[1] All religions are tailored to reflect, be it unknowingly, some aspect of the divine threefoldness. There are religions of the Father and religions of the Spirit. Among the first I would place the traditions which envision God in the pattern of man, as one person with unlimited personality, or as a multitude of persons with limited personalities, where the limitations of each are apparently compensated by their multiplication: this seems to be the dominant tendency, exemplified by the polytheism or animism of most of the early civilisations. There are also religions of the Spirit: God, who somehow extends into and underlies all that is, is without personality. This would be the trend of the great Asian religions, which rely on a more or less avowed pantheism, whether positive as in Hinduism or negative as in Buddhism. A third pattern is provided by the semitic religions, especially in the form illustrated in the Old Testament. These religions of mediation adumbrate what, in Christianity, became the revelation of the Word as Son, of the Second Person, the link between the First and the Third. In this area the "Religions of the Book" appear as religions of the middle way.

Without giving up this overview of religion in light of Trinitarian doctrine, I intend to reflect specifically on the Christian understanding of the Three Persons.

o o o

Christian believers who attempt to formulate the Trinitarian vision of the New Testament, have at their disposal the intellectual apparatus of their culture. But one can easily distinguish three main strands in this culture. One strand derives from the general conceptions of monotheism. Regardless of the historical origins of monotheism, especially in its biblical form, the belief that the realm of the divine,far from being formless or faceless, is centered in one personality for whom most languages have a name, can act as the primary point with which to compare the vision of the Three. This provides an introduction to Trinitarian reflection from a philosophical point of view. In fact, the more philosophical speculations of theologians have been focused upon the apparent conflict between the oneness of God and the threeness of the Father, the Son and the Spirit. Thus Thomas Aquinas canonised a distinction, introduced into scholastic methodology by his master Albertus Magnus, between a tractate de Deo uno, which comes first, and a tractate de Deo trino, which comes second. The basic problem in this case is to investigate how the oneness of the divine nature, encapsulated in one God, is compatible with the threeness of the Christian representation of this one God as Father, Son, and Spirit. Thomas Aquinas could justify this approach with his apologetic concern about Jews and Moslems.[2] Yet this innovation – unknown to Peter Lombard,the father of scholasticism – is questionable. The parallel Franciscan tradition followed the line of Peter Lombard more faithfully. Bonaventure begins his Commentary on the Sentences, bk I,dist. II,with the topic, de sancta Trinitate et Unitate, concerning which one should, he says, "first believe the Trinity, second, understand what is believed, third, formulate what is understood".[3] Yet Aquinas's choice was far from arbitrary: if most of humankind believes in one God, then Christians may be called to justify, at the tribunal of this quasi-universal belief, their Trinitarion addition to the basic monotheism of natural religion.

Such an apologetical and missionary concern

need not rule out other approaches. One can well take as the basic point of reference for Christian doctrine the biblical concept of God. Then, God, though still supremely One, is not a nature. He is a person who, however transcendent in self, acts in Israel - and ultimately among all peoples - within the fabric of history. In relation to this God the primary attitude is not philosophical speculation about the what of divinity, but faithful obedience to the One who manifests himself as God in biblical history. Such a point of departure for Trinitarian doctrine is naturally suggested by the Jewish origins of Christian theology: it is to the Adonai of Hebrew tradition and Jewish experience that Paul relates his vision of the risen Jesus. The Judeo-Christians, orthodox as well as heterodox, lived their Christian faith still in the horizon of Jewish piety; and this brought about a certain hesitancy to break the barriers of monopersonalistic theism. Two ways were open to such a break. One could assert that, besides and from the unpronounceable Name revealed to Moses and known by Jesus as Abba, there also was Another, vaguely known to Jews under the other divine names - Dabar (Word), Hochmah (Sophia, Wisdom) - and that this Other had manifested himself in the flesh as Jesus. Or, more shocking to Jewish conceptions perhaps, yet in tune with the Christian perception of the divine dimension in Jesus, one could identify Jesus as the incarnate form of the One who had revealed himself to Moses; in this case, however, he was not first, since there was also the unknown Father whom Jesus called Abba, to whom he referred as to the source of all he was and the motivation of all he did. In both models the Spirit follows as the Third to whom Jesus points and whom he prays the Father to send as "the other Advocate" (J.14:16). In this perspective, Jesus appears on earth as the Ebed Yahweh, the Son-Servant (pais in Greek) of the Supreme Father and Lord, or - second option - as the Lord himself, Kyrios, revealing the Ultimate Source of divinity, whose perfect image he is.

But another basic point of reference was still

possible. In the complex society of the early Church, made of Jews and Gentiles, the Church had to accommodate, until it could absorb, the differences between Palestinian Jews and diaspora Jews, together with the many brands of pagan culture which flourished in hellenistic society. Paganism itself was not without attempts to express the complexity of the divine simplicity. What had been done formerly through Greek and Roman mythology was now the object of sophisticated initiations through the mystery-cults, of advanced forms of contemplation in the philosophies of Middle-Platonism and Neo-Platonism, of various popular yet deep philosophies in Pythagorism, Stoicism, or Epicurianism. Here, Trinitarian thought had to struggle, not only with a general belief in one God but also with the notion that sparks of divinity, deep within us, shrouded in garments of flesh, cry for liberation. The ascent to God through ritual initiations or mystical experiences is the reverse of the vague, yet fairly general belief of hellenistic paganism, that God sends forth emanations of himself, in which divinity, as it spreads itself, also thins itself out. Gnosticism presented what many may have seen as an attractive alternative to the limitation of divinity to three ...three what? emanations? processions? manifestations? masks? persons? This third point of reference for Trinitarian reflection did not vanish with the religious conceptions of the Roman empire. Each culture develops its own assumptions, tendencies and views regarding the ultimate mystery of life. At any time therefore Christian theologians and other thinkers may attempt a synthesis between the Christian concept of God and the specific religious or irreligious implications of their civilization. Hegel's Trinitarian thought was such an attempt in the nineteenth century, and the Marxist movements of our day derive from it. Carl Jung's psychologisation of the doctrine of the Trinity is another such attempt.[4]

o o o

These three basic models for the concept of God are bound to influence the Trinitarian thought developed under their impact. Although Judeo-Christianity did not last, it left traces in the pais—christology, the angel-christology and the adoptianist christology found in the early Church.[5] But if Jesus becomes Son of God by adoption, then there is no eternal Trinity. However highly one thinks of the nature of the Logos - created, according to Arius, before all else and the medium of all further creation - there is then a nominal, not a real Trinity, since the Word is divine in name only, not in reality. The subordinatianism of the pre-Nicene Fathers itself attempts to safeguard somehow the belief in One Lord which is in tune with basic Jewish monotheism. But gnosticism challenged the Church to explain the origin of the Two - the Word and the Spirit - who are claimed to be God without being the One God.

The forgotten problems of the hellenistic world are not far behind us. It has been generally admitted, since the studies of Théodore de Régnon in 1892-98, that Trinitarian theology follows two fundamental types.[6] The East would identify the oneness of God with the Father, and therefore see the Persons first and the divine nature second. The West, identifying the oneness of God with the divine nature, would see the nature first and the Persons second. Which is the better way? Which should come first in our conceptualization, the nature or the Persons? Whatever the exact details of his analysis, de Régnon hit on a critical question which confronts the Christian doctrine of God. Does our basic concept of God derive from the divine nature of universal religion, or from the One Person active in biblical history? In the first case, Trinitarian doctrine starts from belief in one divine nature. In the second, it originates in belief in the God manifested in the Old Testament. And if one fears that these ways of envisaging the doctrine of the Trinity are outmoded, one can look nearer to us. Hans Küng, in On Being a Christian (New York, 1976), eliminates the Trinitarian conception of God, because he

61

follows too literally the preconceptions of natural theology and natural religion about the divine nature.[7] Or also, as sensitive a theologian as John Cobb, in Christ in a Pluralistic Age, proposes a view of the Trinity that comes closer to Buddhism than to traditional Christian formulation, because he has not overcome the gnostic hurdles in the way of Trinitarian thought. What claims to be a modern progressive stance is often a sequel to very old problems that have not been entirely solved, or to prejudices that have not been overcome.

It is therefore impossible, in our time, to treat the question of the Trinity in abstracto, as a merely theoretical problem. For Trinitarian doctrine is not a theory about God. It emerges in the early Church out of an experience of God in Christ, under the impact of what the early Christians came to know as the Spirit. It is therefore in part, for us, a historical question. But the historian of dogma is likely to be struck by two facts: first, the groping way in which early theologians, up to the Council of Nicaea (325), described and defended Trinitarian conceptions, even before the Greek and Latin terms for Trinity came in current use; second, the variety of speculative theories that developed about the Trinity once the doctrine of the Nicaean Council on the homoousia between the Father and the Word was finally accepted as the standard of orthodox teaching. The long debates which followed Nicaea acted as a transition between the search for orthodoxy and its universalisation. That such a transition - something like sixty years - was needed is not likely to surprise the church historian. The characteristics of the previous and the subsequent eras present much more of a conundrum.

It is not without good reason that ante-Nicene theology often seems puzzling to us. The basic problem was to pass from vision to formulation, from sight to language, from the view - in the proper sense of the term - of God as Three that was obtained from the New Testament, to an intelligible translation of it in language that would be continuous with the New Testament, satisfactory to the mind, and adequate to the experience of God in liturgical worship and in the interior search of Christian gnosis. This problem belonged to the broader context in which semitic conceptions were being translated into hellenistic language. Translation needed to be done without losing the central purpose of the original semitic views, and without distorting it under the impact of popular and academic philosophies or in the light of the mythological and religious conceptions of the Greek world. Here, the three possible points of reference relatively to the concept of God that we have described drew the church Fathers in opposite directions, which were likely to foster conflicting theologies. The problem was of course compounded by the essential difficulty of expressing the divine without falling into distorting anthropomorphisms. Historically, this corresponds to what Bernard Lonergan has called "the way to Nicaea".[8] Following this way would take us through such complex questions as the subordinationism of the pre-Nicene Fathers, the cosmological conception of the Logos, the distinctions between Logos endiathetos and Logos prophorikos, the various forms of modalism, the struggle on two fronts against the monopersonalism of the extreme monarchianists and the tritheism of some defenders of the Three, the nature and causes of Arianism and Semi-Arianism, to say nothing of the Trinitarian implications of christological controversies. The surprise is indeed not that the way to Nicaea was arduous; it is that theologians and bishops, overcoming so many hurdles, were able to get there at all.

The puzzle presented by the period which followed the acceptance of Nicaea is of another kind. Several approaches to the explanation of Trinitarian doctrine emerged after the victory of the Nicaean formulation. One could find reasons for this in the different orientations of Greek and Latin cultures, in the varieties of ethos which distinguished North Africans from Italian or Gallic Christians, in the immense diversifications of

63

the human mind. Furthermore, we face here one of
the fundamental facts about development of doctrine. The rallying of most of the Church around
a given formulation after a period of hesitancy
and debate serves as starting point for further
reflection and interpretation. What was devised
as a hermeneutical principle to sort out doctrine
in fidelity to Scripture - as for instance the
homoousios formula - stands itself in need of interpretation, even before the passing of the generation which has witnessed its adoption. Theologians are thus propelled into a search for a second hermeneutical principle that will guarantee
the correct understanding and application of the
first. In a sense, orthodoxy recedes behind the
perpetual need to interpret its agreed standards,
and therefore to discover standards of reinterpretation.[9] In the case of Trinitarian doctrine,
however, the Church never became unanimous on such
a second principle. If, in the West, something
did for a long time, fulfill the heremeneutical
function of protecting the homoousia of the Three
Persons, it was the psychological analogy investigated by Augustine, underlined by Anselm, and
endorsed, with the further metaphysical precisions
of his analysis of "relations" in God, by Thomas
Aquinas. Yet Augustine was not the man of only
one idea, and most Trinitarian analogies that
could be thought of in his time found their place
in his De Trinitate. The psychological analogy
was not intended by him to be the hermeneutical
principle which it later became. This is precisely
where the puzzle lies: how could the conciliar
orthodoxy of Nicaea, focused on the confession of
homoousia between the Father and the Son, be so
understood that it needed, in the West at least,
to be bolstered up by analogies which were - and
here I anticipate - of a much more dubious character than what the Council had determined?

Be that as it may, the growth of Trinitarian
theology before and after Nicaea is tied to several key concepts, hinges, as it were, around which
thought circles. Historically indispensable to
understand patristic controversies, these concepts

remain theoretically necessary today to conceptualize belief in the Trinity. They do not merely
correspond to accidental aspects of patristic or
medieval reflection. They refer to structures,
types, or models without which the human mind cannot properly translate in intellectual terms the
vision of the Three conveyed by the New Testament
and represented by Christian art in other media.
To these key concepts we will now turn our attention.

o o o

The first indispensable principle is that of
the Monarchy. In its traditional use, this means
that there is "one principle", one originating
power of everything that is. In the Judeo-Christian language of the Epistle of James, 1:17, there
is one "Father of lights, from whom every worth-
while gift comes." In the hellenistic religions,
to affirm the divine Monarchy amounted to defending the logically unimpeachable proposition that
only One can be the Almighty. The Christians could
not pass this opportunity to use the language of
their times. But in so doing they raised a problem. Is the Monarch the divine nature, or the
Father, or the One who is called Lord? Later Western theology will identify omnipotence as an attribute of divine nature. But for the early theology and, it seems to me, already for the New
Testament, the Almighty is identically the Father,
the originating source of all that is, whether uncreated or created. It is the Father of our Lord
Jesus Christ, whom Paul and most of the Greek
Christian writers before Nicaea call o theos, the
God. Of this basic concept John Henry Newman
wrote: "The Principatus of the Father is a great
Catholic truth, and was taught in the Church after
the Nicene Council as well as before."[10] It is
strenuously defended by Tertullian, the initiator
of Latin Trinitarian theology, even in his polemic
against the monarchianism of Praxeas.[11] Monarchianism misunderstands the Monarchy, since, identifying the Son and, by the same token, the Spirit,

with aspects or manifestations of the Father, it removes from the Monarch any subject of monarchic authority. For the classical concept of the Monarchy does not refer primarily to divine authority over creation. The Father is the Monarch even in the divine realm, over the divinity. The orthodox teaching of the Monarchy is therefore exactly opposite to monarchianism and to all forms of modalism: the Word and the Spirit are not aspects or modalities of the Father. They are those in relation to whom the Father, o theos, is Monarch, the only source, origin, and power, the only arche. For this reason of course, subordinatianism was so appealing to the pre-Nicene Fathers: if the Father is the Monarch, then it would seem logical enough that the Son and the Spirit, as subjects of the monarchy, are his subordinates. They are subjects of the Monarch. In the Son as the perfect image of the Father the Monarch leaves his imprint. The Son is the Monarchy in reverse, the mirroring view of it, perfect reception of the Power, total surrender and obedience. But this cannot be subordination. For subordination includes inferiority, and an inferior image of the Father would not be a perfect image. As the perfection of the Father's imprint, the Son cannot be inferior to the Monarch. He can only be the fulness of the Power as received and exercised, just as powerful as the Power, just as perfect as the Monarch. To affirm the Monarchy is therefore not to take anything from the divine dignity of the Son and the Spirit. Rather, the divinity of the Son and the Spirit demands the affirmation of the Monarchy. Only the absolute Monarch, the absolute Father, can put his mark on a Son who is thereby his absolutely perfect Image. But let us be careful: the Father does not hide in himself a latent pattern, a secret model, an unspoken thought, whom the Son follows and mirrors. It is the Son himself, the Word or Logos, who is the pattern, the model and the thought. To say otherwise would posit two Words, unspoken and spoken, or two Sons, unborn and born; and eventually, I suppose, there would have to be two Spirits, with the result that we would be caught in a descending scale of divine emanations following the gnostic model. But to adore the Son as the only self-expression of the Father implies a negative, apophatic understanding – or should we say, a non-understanding? – of the Father. For if the Monarchy is expressed only in the Son, then the Son is the very expression of the Monarchy; the Father is not Monarch by himself, without the Son. There is neither a moment before he becomes Monarch or Father, nor a level of his being anterior to his being Monarch. Likewise and by the same token, there is no Monarchy of the Father that is not expressed in his Word. One could say: the Lordship of the Son expresses, and is the only expression of, the Monarchy of the Father. But one could also say, though more paradoxically: the Father is the Monarch, but the Son is the Monarchy. Without this Monarchy, the Monarch would be pure Void, Abyss, Unbeing waiting for Being to emerge. Thus the Monarchy leads to affirming the exact commensurability between the Father and the Son. It leads, properly understood, to the principle of homoousia.

o o o

This second basic principle of Trinitarian theology was embodied in the credal formula of the First Council of Nicaea: "We believe...in one Lord, Jesus Christ, the Son of God, born of the Father, only-begotten, that is, from the ousia of the Father, God from God, light from light, true God from true God, born, not made, homoousion to the Father..." Authors have not been wanting to defend the proposition that the adoption of this formula in 325 was the single most important event in the first centuries of the Church, perhaps even in its entire doctrinal history so far.[12] For, consecrating the endorsement of a Greek vocabulary for the formulation of the Christian faith, it accepted the principle of doctrinal development. It made possible future developments and the eventual adoption, in other movements of acculturation, of other formulas in other languages. And since today for the first time in Christian history, the

67

Church faces the need to formulate and interpret its doctrines in the many languages of Asia and Africa, a study of homoousios and an understanding of its implication may well be the most urgent task for contemporary believers.

Yet the selection of this term was not without difficulty. The word was borrowed from popular and philosophical language. Popularly, it meant, "made of the same material" and was most unsuitable to speak of God. Philosophically, it could mean many things, depending on how ousia (substance) was understood. As a term often used to express the unity of the human race (men, for the Greeks are homoousioi), it meant, "of the same nature"; its application to the Father and the Son risked suggesting that two Gods share the divine nature. The Fathers at Nicaea needed therefore to agree on a clear theological meaning of the word; and their failure to do so explains to a great extent that the Creed of Nicaea was rejected by many bishops in the post-Nicene debates.

I am not sure, moreover, that the homoousios justifies Bernard Lonergan's description of doctrinal development as a passage from truth understood quoad nos to truth understood quoad se.[13] Pre-Nicene Trinitarian thought had indeed a tendency, exemplified by Justin of Rome, to envision the birth of the Logos prophorikos, of the Word expressed by the Father, in terms of its relation to the creation of the cosmos. Justin could also closely associate the Son and the angels. But the Son thus perceived was not seen only in a cosmological or angelological perspective. He was not only expressive of, but also identical with, the Logos endiathetos, the Word yet unspoken. The problem of Justin, Tatianus and others who distinguished these two aspects of the Logos was concerned with eternity and time. They had difficulty conceptualizing the Logos as other than a movement which, within the Father's eternity, would introduce a difference similar to a time-distinction between before and after. This language did not refer primarily to the Word's rela-

68

tion to human time, quoad nos. It denoted the
Word in relation to God's eternity, quoad se. The
adoption of homoousios marks indeed an awakening
of consciousness in regard to the mystery of God.
But what exactly is the homoousios credal statement designed to make us aware of?

The chief point of the doctrine relates to the
divine ousia (nature, or substance, but the
English language has no exact correspondent to
ousia). It aims at affirming the belief - necessary to safeguard Christian monotheism - that
there is only one divine ousia, one "that" of the
Father and his Word. This ousia is not shared between the Two, for sharing entails dividing, par-
titioning, and would destroy the divine simplicity.
Rather, the divine ousia is at the same time the
total reality of the Father and the total reality
of the Word. On the basis of the Monarchy, one
must say that, the Father being the divine ousia,
the Son is from the Father's ousia, from the God-
ness of the Father. Yet the Son is so from the
Father's God-ness that he himself is the totality
of the God-ness. The Father is God-ness as unori-
ginated and originating; the Son is the same God-
ness as posited in a gift-receiving stance which
originates in the Father. This does not make the
Two into aspects or attributes of the divinity, as
modalists would have it. Neither Fatherhood nor
Sonship is an attribute of the divine nature. But
the attribute of radiance, glory, generosity -
love, we might say - comes to fruition in and as
Father and Son; it differentiates itself in a
movement by which each is the whole ousia. As
attributes of God are no other than God, the Father
is the "that" of God as yet unrelated, though
filled with potentialities for relationships. The
Son is the same "that" as emerging in relationship. As soon as one understands the divine ousia
as self-giving love, one perceives something of
the Father and the Son. Total love giving itself,
yearning for an object to be given to, for a subject in which to inhere: this is the Father. Total
love received, given, expressed, and therefore expressive: this is the Son. That such an inner

differenciation is compatible with perfect unity, without separation and without confusion, is implied in the homoousia of the Son with the Father.

This homoousia enables us to make another important point. What kind of Fatherhood do we ascribe to the Father? In order to maintain the utter transcendence of God over any kind of human fatherhood, it is not necessary, although it is useful, to proceed through the detailed analysis of analogy of proper proportionality. For already the transcendence of the Father as Father is affirmed by the Nicaean dogma without an explicit philosophy of analogy. Human fatherhood, the only one of which we have direct experience, - some of us by being parents, all of us by being children to human fathers - makes father and child, not only distinct from, but also unlike, each other. The child is not what the father is; and psychoanalysis has taught us that the failure to recognize the autonomy of the child lies at the source of most psychic disorders. Parent and offspring are separate individuals who can well, once the need for protection of the child has passed, ignore each other. They both participate in the one human nature; they do not have one and the same ousia in the Nicaean sense of the term. On this point one should not be misled by the formula of the Council of Chalcedon (451): Jesus Christ is "homoousios with the Father in divinity, homoousios with us in humanity".[14] This is notoriously ambiguous, since the first homoousios is Nicaean, while the second has another meaning familiar to hellenistic philosophy. In God, the Son is what the Father is. A hypothetical onlooker who would not know of the Son's origin could not possibly discern any distinction between the Father and his Image. "He who sees me sees the Father"(John 14:9) clearly expresses the homoousia of the Father and the Son. Divine Fatherhood is not at all adequately represented by human fatherhood. A human father is not an image of the Father in heaven who was revealed in Jesus's relationship to him. The Father is not a heavenly model for human fatherhood. In the light of the homoousios dogma, Fatherhood in God should be understood eminently in relation, not to human fathers, but to human children's love for their parents. Rather than the reality of the First, it denotes directly the human response of love to the revelation of the Monarchy. Thus homoousia allows us to use the language of fatherhood to connote, by contrast, the uniqueness of the Father.

But if the term, homoousios, was selected at Nicaea to designate the Word who is from the Father, the Second Council of Constantinople, in 553, extended it to the Trinity as such, the "Triada homoousion".[15] For there are not only Two, but Three, and the Three are one, in homoousia.

o o o

That God is believed to be Three in homoousia makes it necessary to posit a third principle, which I will call the principle of derivation. The Son derives from the Father as Word, Image, Wisdom. To express this derivation, theology borrowed the word "procession" from the speculations of the Valentinian gnostics.[16] For it is not the origin of words that matters for orthodoxy, but their use. This procession or derivation - the Word derives from the Father - is total when seen in the Son. This is the perfect Image. The only way to discern the Father is to see the Son, such a "seeing" being of course a phenomenon of second sight, of faith, and neither the exercise of our sense organs nor the insight of our intellect. Yet when seen in the Father, in the source, the derivation is not exhaustive. There is no seeing of the Father, even in faith, for of the Father one can only see his self-expression, the Son. Seeing, in this case, means discerning the Father from what his reflected Image shows. It is inferring from experience as to what lies beyond experience. The Source is inexhaustible even in its perfect derivation into the stream which we call the Word. Were the Source exhaustible, there would ultimately be nothing left to be reflected by the Image; the ousia would have self-emptied and the Son would be without consistence; the Word would have no content.

The bibical expression of this principle is the doctrine of the Spirit. If the Father is not emptied by the derivation of the Son, then another derivation is possible. This one cannot follow the same way, for then it would be identical with the first derivation, and the Two who derive from the Father would be only one. The Christian tradition has therefore distinguished them by talking of generation in the first case and simply of procession, or spiration, in the second. Many theologians, envisioning the two derivations in their one source, have seen the first, not as initiating, yet as carrying already in itself the movement of the second derivation. Thus Augustine, and after him the great mass of Latin theology, speak of the Spirit as proceeding from the Father and the Son as from one principle (tanquam ab uno principio).[17] Others, envisaging the two derivations in their unique source as one stream with double effect, have liked to see them as one divine sophia, the expressed and expressive aspect of the ousia.[18]

Formulations of these two derivations have been many. This should surprise no one. For besides the theological necessity of speaking, Christians have needed doxological formulas expressive of Trinitarian piety. The Church has spoken of the Father, the Son and the Spirit; the Father, through the Son, in the Spirit; the Spirit, from the Father through the Son; the Spirit, from the Father and the Son; the Spirit, from the Father alone. Excited discussions have taken place between upholders of one or the other formula. Yet much of the debate, it seems to me, had been off the point, since there cannot be an adequate formula for the divine mystery. The point is to maintain, together with the homoousia of the Three, the derivation of Two from the First. For it is this derivation which enables us to distinguish the Three. Without it, homoousia would only be a complicated way of saying that God is one.

This helps us to understand the drift of Trinitarian controversies in the fourth and fifth centuries. Discussion centered on the Son before being extended to the Spirit. The Church passed from Nicaea I in 325 (the Son is homoousios with the Father) to Constantinople I in 381 (the Spirit is co-adored and con-glorified with the Father and the Son). The affirmation of the Third completes the affirmation of the First and the Second by emphasizing that the First is not emptied by the derivation of the Second. The First remains the total ousia as such, ready for communication though not communicated, unoriginate, and self-existent. The Second is the total ousia as communicated, received, self-affirming, expressing, imaging, and other-existent. The Spirit also is the total ousia, non-exhausted by the first derivation, still entirely filled with self, even, so to say, enriched by its passage to self-affirmation, and now self-enabled to express itself further, indefinitely, infinitely. Because the Spirit is the fulness of divinity despite the total self-expression of the Father in the Son, the divine ousia, having lost none of its Power, can further extend its self-expression - and still in other ways than in the divine derivations - into the creative act by which the universe is called into being.

Following the hesychast debates in the fourteenth century, Eastern Orthodox theology has also expressed the principle of the inexhaustiveness of the divine derivations in terms of eternal "energies", the Three being both ousia and power, essence and action.[19] These are not additional derivations within God. They are the two derivations themselves when perceived as the outgoing movement of divinity, the inner movement being the invisible ousia, the other side, the unperceivable aspect of the Three who coinhere in one another. Here again, it is not helpful to cavil about formulations of the mystery, as long as the principle is maintained: as God derives from God, God remains unemptied. The Third is necessary for the integrity of the Second, who is necessary for the

fulness of the First. But let us not delude ourselves; no formulation of the mystery gives us inside knowledge. What we reach is only the surface,
the energies, the sophia. God in himself as ousia
remains unknown.

o o o

Nevertheless, Christian piety and faith need
to speak. They have to find terms, "not so," as
Augustine wrote, "that we may talk, but lest we
remain dumb."[20] We thus come to the fourth Trinitarian principle, the principle of personhood. It
took a great deal of time and a considerable
amount of debate for the Fathers of the Church to
arrive at a consensus on what could be the most
adequate vocabulary to designate the Three. Greek
and Latin terms that we translate as persons were
finally accepted: prosopon, hypostasis, persona,
subsistentia; and the oneness of the divinity was
called ousia, physis, substantia (usually translated as essence, substance, or nature). Evidently
no translation is entirely adequate, either to
what those words are intended to say about God, or
even to what they commonly mean in their own language, since no two languages are completely iso-
topic. But whatever the limitations of terms, the
intention is to express the faith that there is
"that" in God which must be designated as one (one
ousia, substantia, nature), while the same "that"
must also be designated as three (three hypostas-
eis, personae, persons.) The influence of St.
Athanasius was capital in the eventual endorsement
of ousia and homoousios by the whole church; and
the Cappadocian Fathers, especially Gregory Nazianzen, were largely responsible for the acceptance
of the vocabulary for persons. But three qualifications need to be kept in mind when we use
these terms.

Firstly, the word person and the equivalent
nomenclature of other languages are not to be
applied univocally to the Three. The Father is
not the kind of Person that the Son is, nor is the

74

Spirit the kind of Persons that the Father and the Son are. Since Person designates what specifies the Father as Father, the Son as Son, the Spirit as Spirit, the Three Persons are also three personhoods. There is not one divine personality with three aspects or applications. There are three utterly different centers or foci in God which are, for convenience's sake, designated by the common term, person. But they are so different that in 1442 the Council of Florence, following the theology of the scholastics, could speak of "opposition" in its famous formula: (in God) "all are common except where there is an opposition of relation". [21] Persons were understood as "relations of opposition". The Father and the Son are opposed, in the sense, as it were, of being face to face. And the Spirit corresponds to another kind of opposition to, of face to face with, the Father (Latin theology adding, and the Son).

Secondly, as in the case of all terms used to speak of the mystery of God, the word Person cannot have in relation to the Three the meaning it has in human experience. It is even quite misleading to speak of three Persons if we have in mind three individuals. Personality, especially in English usage, can denote no more than individuality. With such a meaning, it should not be used of the Father, the Son, the Spirit. Yet Person, especially in the languages derived from Latin (like French, Italian, Spanish), also has another connotation: it designates the human being as profoundly involved in relationships with others. In this sense, there is no human person separate from others. Personhood is constituted by interpersonal relationships. Human self-awareness is always a consciousness of self in interaction with other selves. This sense of the word is much more helpful when we think of the divine persons. At least it makes us realize that each divine Person is Person in relation to the others, that no one of the Three can be posited in isolation. This was already Augustine's understanding: persons, he specified, are ad invicem (turned toward one another), not ad semetipsum (turned toward self). [22]

75

This justifies using one word, person, for three different personhoods. Whatever the difference between the Three, one point is identical: each is in relationship with the others, and this relationship constitutes its unique characteristic as a Person.

Thirdly, each Person, one may say, represents a "how" of God, a stance, an attitude, a position. The Three are not successive stances, as though God was successively Father, Son, and Spirit. They are simultaneous, each and all necessary and sufficent to the fulness of the divine ousia. But let us not think of each Person as other than the ousia. The "that" or "what" of each is the "that" or "what" of God. The content of divine Fatherhood is no other than the content of divine Filiation or of divine Spirithood. The Threeness of God is not superadded to Oneness. It is the Oneness, which can be One only as Three just as the Threeness can be Three only as One. There are not three divine ousiai, but one. And this ousia, the divine essence or substance, is the Father, is the Son, is the Spirit, and is each of the Three in and by a certain attitude in regard to the other Two.

Because of the need to underline these qualifications of the term person as applied to God, theologians have attempted to provide clear definitions of the term. One stream of tradition derives from the definition proposed by Boethius: person is naturae rationalis individua substantia (an individual substance as individuated, as made an individual).23 Because of the ambiguity of defining a divine Person as an individual, Thomas Aquinas modified the definition, which became: person is subsistens distinctum in natura rationali (that which subsists as distinct in a rational nature). Then, person is that which is, insofar as it is distinct from others and rational. It belongs to the order of subsistence (the hypostasis of the Greeks, in its older sense), of essence as subsisting. This line of thought makes it clear that the Person is no other than the divine essence (ousia), the "that", as connoted by a specific "how".

To the twelfth century theologian and mystic, Richard of St Victor, we owe a different approach: person is intellectualis naturae incommunicabilis existentia (an incommunicable existence of the divine nature).[24] Here, person pertains to the order of existence, of "how" rather than of "what"; it resides in what is incommunicable, unique and proper to each. The Father communicates all of himself to the Son, but for being the Father; and all of himself to the Spirit, but for being originator of both the Son and the Spirit. The one God is three Existants. This line of thinking was preserved by the theologians of the Franciscan tradition. The definition adopted by Jean Calvin pertains to the same line of thought: a Person is "a residence in the essence of God, which, referred to the others, is distinct from them with an incommunicable property".

Set at the level of existence, the notion of person holds together the two horns of the dilemma: person is "referred to the others" and yet remains "incommunicable". A more modern perspective could say: the unity of one person exists only within the unity of two persons in love; but the unity of two persons in love exists only - in the case of men and women, within the unity of humankind, - in God, within the unity of the Third Person. It is not accidental that Richard of St Victor, with his understanding of personhood, describes the derivation of the Three in terms of love: they are amans, delectus and condilectus. For love is self-giving or it is not (bonum diffusivum sui: "good spreads itself around"). The dilectio (love) which the Father is, is given to a well-beloved (dilectus), and, as it cannot rest in the well-beloved without ceasing to give itself, it flows on into a condilectus who is mutually loved by the Father and the Son: the Spirit. But Aquinas, given his understanding of personhood, does not feel at home in the love analogy, and therefore prefers the psychological language: substance - thought - will.

The Son proceeds from the substance of the Father by way of Thought; the Spirit proceeds by way of Will.[25]

o o o

One could undoubtedly go to great lengths attempting to perfect the Trinitarian vocabulary. Such attempts have not been wanting in the Catholic tradition. But the Reformers in general were wary of speculating on what Luther called, in the Schmalcald Articles, "the high articles of the Majesty of God".[26] Melanchthon even went to the extreme of eliminating such questions from his systematic theology, the Loci communes (1521), under the pretext that "the mysteries of divinity we have the more rightly adored than investigated". Calvin, extremely selective in his vocabulary and careful to speculate only to the extent needed to clarify his position, wisely recommends discretion: "Here, as indeed elsewhere in the recondite mysteries of Scripture, one must philosophize soberly and with great moderation, with great care lest thought or tongue trespasses beyond the limits of the Word of God."[27] Such a warning remains timely. Yet one cannot ignore all speculative investigations. For we cannot truly grasp to what extent reflection on the Trinity lies at the heart of Christian faith unless we realize its place in the life and thought of the great Christian thinkers.

These two aspects of Trinitarian belief, which I call life and thought, cannot be separated in the case of St Augustine of Hippo, to whom we owe the most complete investigation of Trinitarian doctrine in patristic times. But his De Trinitate does not stand alone in Augustine's production.[28] His entire itinerary to God leads him to the De Trinitate. From his literary or philosophical conversion when, already disquiet in his Manichaean beliefs, he read Cicero's Hortensius in Milan, through his deeper religious conversion by way of Neo-Platonism, Augustine was prepared for a progressive discovery, under the influence of Ambrose of Milan and of his own mother Monica, of two fundamental structures of Christian experience: the Trinity as the "region of resemblance", the goal and purpose of life, the patria or homeland, and Christ, the incarnate Word, as the example and the via, the way to the Three Persons.

In the typology suggested at the beginning of the present chapter, Augustine's basic problem arose from a confrontation of the Christian proclamation - at first as Ambrose preached it, then as Augustine himself discovered it by meditating on Scripture - with the gnostic concerns of his own culture. In his case, gnosticism took the form of Manichaeanism. Augustine believed for several years that the Manichaean teachers would lead him to understand the divine light which is suffused in all things. Instead, he found that this was a mystification. By defending a materialist concept of God and by dividing the divine into good and evil, Manichaeanism could explain neither the material nor the spiritual universe. The Neo-Platonists, meanwhile, presented a higher perspective. They proposed an interior ascent to the True, the Good, the One, whom Augustine, in his passage to Christianity, had no difficulty identifying as Truth, Charity, Eternity. These are attributes of God; but they connote, besides dimensions or qualities of the divine nature, also those whom Augustine effectively came to identify as the Word of God, the Charity or Spirit of God, and the eternal Father.

Augustine was enabled to go beyond the neo-platonist vision by his discovery, around 488 at Thagaste, in North Africa, of the doctrine of creation, unknown to hellenistic thought.[29] If God is the Creator, then a divine imprint has been left on the universe, made, in the words of the book of Wisdom, XI, 21, according to "measure, number and weight". Since "measure, number, weight" ensure the interior unity of each creature, Augustine can now understand creation in the light of Trinitarian doctrine - and Trinitarian doctrine also in the light of creation. All creatures are made by the one God, who is "Supreme Measure, supreme Number, supreme Order".[30] But the divine imprint has also marked the human creature. And since Augustine has been convinced of the spirituality of man by neo-platonism, he seeks for the image of the Trinity in the human soul. The soul, which can say, "I am, I think, I will," experiences itself as being, thought and will; it thereby can know itself as the image of what being, thought and will are in God, that is, attributes which connote Persons, the Father, the Word, the Spirit.

The fifteen books of the De Trinitate investigate this interior image. After studying some questions raised by the missions of the Word and the Spirit into the created world in relation to the oneness of God (books I-IV), Augustine examines the personal relations and the one substance of God (books V-VII), and finally, in the main section of his work, diverse formulations of the "psychological theory" (books VIII-XV). The psychological theory, often considered to be Augustine's chief contribution to Trinitarian theology, has had considerable influence on later Western conceptions. But it is usually misrepresented. It is not enough to sum it up in the idea that Augustine finds God's image in the three spiritual faculties of the soul, memory, intellect, will. For this seems to convey a simplistic view of God as a divine substance with three faculties. Augustine in fact proposes several forms of the image, and chiefly four: the lover, that which is loved, and love (amans, et quod amatur, et amor); the mind, its love, and its knowledge of its love (mens, et amor, et notitia ejus); the mind, its knowledge, its love (mens, notitia, dilectio); memory, intellect, and will (memoria, intelligentia, voluntas). And when he finds the last to be the most adequate, Augustine remains well aware that this does not provide a true knowledge of what God is. The psychological theory does not explain the Trinity. It explains how we, as human beings, can experience the Trinity in the exercise of our spiritual faculties. It provides a scale of ascent to God, up more and more adequate formulations of the image of God in us. For the formulations correspond to higher and higher forms of this image. Augustine's investigation does not primarily build an analogical scale to enable the mind better to conceive the Trinity. It is first and chiefly an anagogical ascent toward beatitude, through experiencing God, in faith and love, as Word and as Love, and thereby also as the Father who speaks and who loves.

o o o

That Augustine's psychological analogy for the Trinity has dominated Western reflection over the last few centuries is largely due to Thomas Aquinas, who went beyond Augustine in making it the chief analogy for our attempt to understand the Three Persons. Yet Thomas's more original contribution to the theory of the Trinity lies elsewhere, namely in his adoption of the Aristotelian category of "relation" to explain the Persons.

One finds two main approaches to Trinitarian theology in the works of Aquinas. The Summa contra gentes, written to enable the Dominican colleagues of Aquinas to argue with Jews and Moslems, assumes that the Father is already known: this is the one God equally recognized by Jews and by Moslems. The argumentation tries to show that the attributes of thought and of will are, in this one God or Father, more than qualities: they are Persons, the one proceeding from the Father along the lines of thought by a sort of intellectual emergence, the other proceeding from the same Father along the lines of love. In this proceeding or procession the divinity relates to itself in a way which, being itself divine, must be self-subsistent. Thus, not only the Father, but also the Word or Son and the Spirit, should be recognized as ways of self-subsistence, or Persons, of the one divine Substance. That these ways of self-subsistence, far from being mere views of the mind, are really distinct relationships within God is conceivable if

81

we reflect, with Aristotle, that the ways in which persons relate to one another are not accidental to them. If the category of the relational in human experience is quite special, in that it is neither essential nor accidental to one's being, neither necessary nor expendable, one may conceive that, in the divine simplicity where nothing is accidental, relations should be themselves substantial. [31]

The main step in the development of St. Thomas's Trinitarian thought is taken when, in the Summa theologica, the Three Persons are defined, in the logic already of what Thomas had written in the Contra gentes, as substantial relations: "Because a relation, insofar as it is something real in God, is the (divine) essence itself, and the essence is identical with the person (as is clear from q. 39, a.1.), it is appropriate that a relation be identical with a person." [32] Thus, in the full Thomist conception, the divine Persons are not terms related to one another by thought and by love, as popular exposés of Thomism tend to suggest. Rather, the Persons are the divine essence, or substance, relating to itself in such a way that these relationships are constituted as self-subsistent: the Father is Fatherhood, the Son is Filiation, the Spirit is Spiration. Fatherhood and Filiation stand in necessary togetherness, since each is needed for the other to be what it is. Likewise Fatherhood-Filiation, acting as one principle, and Spiration stand in necessary togetherness, for each is needed for the other to be what it is. Here, as one can see, Thomas Aquinas incorporates the doctrine of the Filioque into his Trinitarian conception.

The divine Persons are thus identified with Relations, which themselves come to be by means of Processions from the Father along the ways of Thought and of Will. In the Summa theologica the approach to this theology is made easier by the starting point: this time, Thomas argues from what is previously believed, not of God as Father, but of God as divine nature. Only after investigating at length the nature of God (I, q. 2-26) does he ask: are there processions in God (q.27)? The rest follows logically: are there relations in God (q.28)? are there persons in God (q.29)? Consideration of each Person follows (q.30-38). The tractate ends with a comparative study of the different concepts used and of some other traditional problems (q.39-43).

Undoubtedly, this overview of Thomist Trinitarian theology does not do justice to the nuances and the depth of the demonstration. But my ambition, for the moment, is modest: I only wish to show that the theology of the Processions-Relations-Persons as developed by Thomas Aquinas and adopted ever since by most Roman Catholic theologians, is not on a par with the central tradition on the doctrine of the Trinity. The impressive speculative achievement of St Thomas has been made at the double cost of tying explanation of the Christian faith in the Trinity to a particular philosophy, and of absolutizing the psychological analogy. St Thomas's doctrine is also hampered by his definition of person as subsistens distinctum in natura rationali. The tendency to individualizing each Person, which this definition entails, is counterbalanced by his further identification of personhood with relation. But there results a disharmony between two views of the divine Persons. These are "subsisting distinctly" in the divine nature and thus are logically distinct from the nature. Yet they are also identical with the relations of this nature to itself. Above all, whereas Thomas's analogical reflection about the Trinity remains an inexhausted source of intellectual wonder, one misses the anagogical accent which was so clear with Augustine. This accent, on the contrary, dominates the Trinitarian theology of St. Thomas's contemporary, Bonaventure.[33] And this is due, I suspect, to St. Thomas's preference for the psychological analogy, while Bonaventure prefers Richard's analogy of dilectio. One can hardly feel religiously involved in speculation on the intellect and the will. But the analysis of love touches human persons to their very depths.

83

o o o

Compared with the previous tradition, modern
theology has been immensely impoverished by Schleiermacher's relegation of Trinitarian thought to
the conclusion of his influential volume, The
Christian Faith (1821). In Schleiermacher's perspective, the doctrine of the immanent Trinity
(concerning interrelationships in God) is only a
theological inference from Christian experience.
It combines with belief in one God the twofold
awareness of the divine dimension in Christ and of
the presence of the Spirit in the Church. But in
this case one cannot truly speak of the Trinity as
being revealed: it is only concluded from the
Christian self-consciousness, as this has developed in the Church in the light of the redemption
through Christ. Schleiermacher finds in the tension between the concepts of equality and of gra-
dation a sign that the doctrine is still in an unfinished state.

Under Schleiermacher's influence, much of recent theology has returned to a purely economic
Trinity (God in relation to us).[34] This has been
updated in relation to the economic Trinity of the
early Church, in that economy is described in psychological rather than cosmological terms. By the
same token, Trinitarian doctrine is subjected to
the fluctuations and vagaries of psychological
theories.

Yet Schleiermacher's problem, whatever we
think of his unfinished solution, has remained
with us: how can Trinitarian doctrine be formulated in modern terms? Cyril Richardson, followed
by many, simply gave up the doctrine; for him,
"the terms", i.e. Father, Son, Spirit," are ways
of thinking about God from different points of
view."[35] But if Christianity abandons what has
characterized its concept of God from the beginning, why should it continue to differ from the
great monotheistic religions? Why does it not become a form of Judaism or a form of Islam? Paul
Tillich understood the three personal names,Father,

Son, Spirit, as symbols of three dimensions of being, for which he used several words: there is
Power or Ground or Abyss; there is Existence or
Form or Meaning; there is Life or Unity. But such
a description makes the three persons into "moments within the process of the divine life",[36]
tones down the importance of the Nicaean homoousios, and tends to Sabellianism: the Persons are
aspects of the human awareness of God, rather than
distinct realities in God. Karl Barth, attempting
to reformulate and strengthen traditional orthodoxy, wished to find a better term than person.
Failing to discover one, he suggested that the
three persons should be understood as three "distinctive modes of being". This avoids modalism
because these modes of being are not in our minds
only, but are really, and really distinct, in
God.[37] With the same concern and in the same line,
Karl Rahner has opted for three "manners of subsisting", which "says simply the same as the definition of 'person' in St Thomas, and the same as
the corresponding Greek word".[38]

I do not myself find these suggestions very
helpful. I suspect that they are prompted by the
individualistic connotations of the term person in
Germanic languages, while the Latin languages
stress its interpersonal implications. Yet a modern rendering is not impossible. Three "dimensions" of the divine being may be too physical an
analogy for many readers. Yet it can be accept-
able to those who are aware of the non-spatial
meaning of dimensionality in modern mathematics
and physics. There are three dimensions of God:
the dimension of depth, abyss, the absolute, the
ultimate; the dimension of verticality out of the
depth; the dimension of horizontality spreading
out the verticality. Here again, dimension varies
in meaning as it is used of each of the Three. If,
as in Karl Heims's theology, God as divine nature
is a supra-polar dimension of reality,[39] there are
three inner dimensions of otherness within it,
three foci of the one divine Self. This is borrowed from the analogy of light, already used by
the council of Nicaea itself, in whose creed it is

85

embodied.

There are three foci or centers of divine self-consciousness: the focus of divine self-sufficiency, autonomy, unorigination, darkness, silence, in which light is self-emptying and dazzling: this is the Father; the focus of divine self-expression, fulness, communication, word, wisdom, filiation, in which light is illuminating: this is the Son; the focus of divine self-possession, self-appropriation, movement, victory, peace, transforming power, love, in which light is all-encompassing: this is the Spirit. The divine nature or substance or ousia is that which is common to the three centers of divine self-consciousness: they are conscious of an identical content, the lighthood of the light. These divine centers or foci are radically and essentially related to one another: essentially, in that they are awareness of the same divinity; radically, in that the Second and the Third originate in the First. The Second results from the self-projection of the first, its passage from silence to speech, from darkness to illumination. The Third results from the First's gathering up into the one divine Self all that has been expressed in the Second.

In any case, theological reflection has a limited scope in relation to the Trinitarian concept of God. It attempts to account intellectually or rationally for what is much more immediately self-evident than any reasoning can make it. For a vision, when it is apprehended, needs no other justification than itself. Faith in the Holy Trinity is a vision, an insight, it reveals the inscape of God. It opens a door through which those who enter are led, not into knowing or undering God, but truly into God. Analogy, as it can be handled by theological reflection, finds its purpose in anagogy. It is to the mystics that we should now turn to learn about the Three Persons.

1. La Religion à l'épreuve des idées modernes, Paris, 1970, p. 96-102.

2. This concern is evident in the Summa contra gentes, where the Trinity is explained in bk IV, ch. 1-26, following a long treatise on the one God, bk I, ch. 10-102. St Thomas's main tractate on the Trinity, in Summa theologica, I, q. 27-43, also follows the treatise on the one God, q. 2-26.

3. See also Bonaventure's Disputed Questions on the Trinity, in Opera omnia, vol. V, Quaracchi, 1891, p. 45-115, or in Obras de San Buenaventura, vol. V, (Biblioteca de Auctores Cristianos, Madrid, 1948) p. 94-306.

4. Carl Jung: A Psychological Approach to the Trinity, in Collected Works, vol. 11, 2nd ed., Princeton, 1969, p. 109-200.

5. Jean Daniélou: Théologie du Judéo-Cristianisme, Paris, 1958, p. 169-255.

6. Théodore de Régnon: Etudes de théologie positive sur la Sainte Trinité, 4 vol., Paris, 1898.

7. Hans Küng: On Being a Christian, New York, 1976, p. 472-478; John Cobb: Christ in a Pluralistic Age, Philadelphia, 1975. For other denials of the doctrine of the Trinity, see below, note 35.

8. Bernard Lonergan: The Way to Nicea. The Dialectical Development of Trinitarian Theology, Philadelphia, 1976.

9. This evidently poses the problem of development of doctrine. I have written on this question in La Théologie parmi les sciences humaines, Paris, 1975, p. 151-56; La Tradition au XVIIe siècle, Paris, 1969, p. 493-512; The Seventeenth-century Tradition, Leiden, 1978, p. 197-218; 248-251.

10. John Henry Newman: Tracts Theological and Ecclesiastical, London, 1908, p. 167.

11. Joseph Moingt: Théologie trinitaire de Tertullien, 3 vol., Paris, 1966.

12. John Courtney Murray: The Problem of God, New Haven, 1964, p. 31-60.

13. Lonergan, op. cit., p. 1-17; 127-37; Method in Theology, New York, 1972, p. 305-324.

14. D.-S., 301; C. O. D., p. 62.

15. D.S., 421; C. O. D., p. 90.

16. Antonio Orbe: Estudios Valentinianos, 5 vol., Rome, 1956-1966.

17. St Augustine: De Trinitate, bk XV, ch. 14 (P. L., 42:920-21).

18. In his own peculiar vocabulary, largely influenced by neo-platonism, Marius Victorinus identifies the Son and the Spirit as two in one Logos, who jointly face the Father or Deus (Adversus Arium, I, 49, in op. cit., p. 340-43). Among recent authors, see Sergius Boulgakof: The Wisdom of God. A Brief Summary of Sophiology, New York, 1937.

19. See below, ch. 4, note 8.

20. St Augustine: De Trinitate, bk V, ch. 9 (P. L., 42:918).

21. D.-S., 1330; C. O. D., p. 546-47.

22. De Trinitate, VII, vi, 11 (P.L., 42:943).

23. Boethius: De personis et duabus naturis, ch. 3 (P. L., 64:1343C); Thomas Aquinas: S. Th., I, q. 30, a. 3-4.

24. De Trinitate, IV, ch. 22 (S. Chr., 63); Bonaventure: Commentary on the Sentences, I, D. XXIII, q. 1; John Duns Scot: Opus Oxoniense, I, D. XXIII, q. unica. See William of Ockham: Commentary on the Sentences, I, D. XXV, q. 1; Jean Calvin: Institu-

tion chrétienne, I, ch. 13, n. 6. The French word, résidence, is Calvin's translation of subsistentia in the Latin text of his work. Melanchthon defines person as subsistens vivum, individuum, intelligens, incommunicabile, non sustentatum ab alio ("something which is, and is living, individual, intelligent, incommunicable, and is not inherent in another") (Examen ordinandorum, 1559, in Corpus Reformatorum, XXIII, col. 2-3, Brunswick, 1855). Based on the Boethian-Thomist line (self-subsistence and individuality), this omnibus description incorporates the heart of the Victorine-Franciscan approach (incommunicability).

25. S. Th., I. q.27, a. 4-5. St Thomas also speaks of "the name of the Spirit, which is Love" (q. 37) and uses the love analogy. But the Spirit is then personalized as amor or dilectio, not as condilectus. This is in line with the Thomist identification of person with relation.

26. Schmalcald Articles, part I (The Book of Concord, Philadelphia, 1959, p. 291-92); C. L. Hill, ed.: The Loci Communes of Philip Melanchthon, Boston, 1944, p. 67.

27. Institution chrétienne, I, ch. 2, n. 21.

28. The fifteen books of the De Trinitate were not composed at one stretch or in their present order. Book VII seems to have come first; books II-IV seem to date from around 412; book XI from 417; the remaining books were composed after 419. See A.-M. de la Bonnardière: Recherches de chronologie augustinienne, Paris, 1965; Oliver du Roy: L'Intelligence de la foi en la Trinité selon saint Augustin, Paris, 1966.

29. I follow here Olivier du Roy's account of Augustine'e early itinerary (op. cit., p. 309-67).

30. De Genesi contra Manichaeos, bk I, 16, 26 (P. L., 34:185).

31. Summa contra gentes, bk IV, ch. 1-26.

32. S. Th., I, q. 40, a. 1.

33. See Titus Szabo: De SS. Trinitate in creaturis refulgente Doctrina S.Bonaventurae, Rome, 1955.

34. See Claude Welch: In This Name. The Trinity in Contemporary Theology, New York, 1953.

35. Cyril Richardson: The Doctrine of the Trinity, New York, 1958, p. 145; here, Richardson returns to the modalism or Sabellianism which had been carefully shunned by the Church Fathers. Among other recent authors who have rejected, or expressed doubts about, the doctrine of the Trinity one finds the Anglican G.W.H. Lampe: God as Spirit, Oxford, 1977. Lampe opines that this doctrine is "in the end less satisfactory than the unifying concept of God as Spirit" (p. 228). Since most religions conceive of God as Spirit, one fails to see how this can do justice to the originality of the Christian experience of God. Lampe's detailed critique of Trinitarian doctrine (p. 206-228) is too incoherent to be serious. Without rejecting the doctrine as such, Hans Küng thinks that it "unfortunately is scarcely understood by modern man" (op. cit., p. 472). He therefore wishes to demythologize it and to explain it simply as an expanded version of belief in the divine presence: "God the Father 'above me', Jesus as the Son and brother 'beside' me, the Spirit of God and Jesus Christ 'in' me" (op. cit., p. 476). But one should ask: does this do justice to the vision of the Three as presented in the New Testament and as contemplated in the Church? I believe it does not.

36. Paul Tillich: Systematic Theology, vol. 2, Chicago, 1957, p. 138-45; A History of Christian Thought, New York, 1968, p. 68-79; Tavard: Paul Tillich and the Christian Message, New York, 1962, p. 113-27.

37. Church Dogmatics, I/1, Edinburgh,1975, p. 348-83; see Eberhard Jüngel: The Doctrine of the Trinity. God's Being is in Becoming, Grand Rapids, 1976.

90

38. Karl Rahner: The Trinity, New York, 1970, p. 110.

39. Karl Heim: Christian Faith and Natural Science, New York, 1957.

IV

The Experience

Seeking for the divine Persons in the work of scholastic or other theologians may be immensely satisfying to the intellect, even if one cannot fully grasp all the fine points of Trinitarian doctrine. But is this true knowledge of God? Such knowledge should be "real and not only notional."[1] It should involve one's whole life and one's whole strength. Precisely, the traditional shape of the Christian liturgy has presupposed a religious awareness rather than a rational description or definition of the Three.[2] From the early time of the Didachè to the liturgical reforms of the Second Vatican Council, the anaphora, or canon of the mass, has followed the threefold pattern: worship of the Father, through the Son, in the Spirit. The Father is addressed in the preface, and the trisagion or sanctus is prayed to him. The Beloved Son is evoked in the account of the last supper, during which the words of consecration are proclaimed over bread and wine. The Spirit is invoked to transform our gifts, in the prayer which has been called the epiclesis by oriental authors. That worship and Trinitarian beliefs are intimately connected appears also in the history of dogma. It was in order to justify the doxologies in use in his liturgy that St Basil wrote his treatise on the Holy Spirit. And the Carolingian discussions of the doctrine of the Trinity were sparked by liturgical differences between the Latins and the Greeks.

Insofar as it is shaped by worship, the Christian life is therefore itself Trinitarian. It implies, whether one is aware of it or not, a sort of participation in the very life of the Three Persons. In worship, and also at many points of theological reflexion and of spiritual meditation, the Trinity and human experience are so interlaced that even a modest awareness of spiritual realities seems to be steeped in God's interpersonal relationships. The classical conception of grace

93

as participation, the analysis of the three theological virtues of faith, love and hope, the theory of the seven gifts of the Holy Spirit, the less well known conception of the twelve beatitudes found among medieval authors: all these investigations of the life of grace imply a direct involvement of the Christian soul with God as Three. The threefoldness of the divine comes to light even as it is mirrored at many other levels of human experience: the structure of friendship and love, the sacramentality of marriage, the dimensions of art and poetry, the inner shape of language, the dialectics of insight and knowing, the unfolding of society and socialization constitute experimental icons where it has been possible for Christian imagination to discern the imprint of the Three.

Yet this itself could remain purely formal. It is not enough to know that my life and that of humankind, by their being rooted in interpersonal relations and in the intercreaturely relations of cosmic ecology, relate us to the Tri-une God, that the liturgy has such and such a shape, that the apparatus of the spiritual life has been described in such and such a way, that the life of the soul follows a threefold pattern, or even that the image of God in me reflects God's triune life. I have sought for a more direct testimony: I have interrogated the mystics.

o

As a supremely vivid realization of the presence and action of God in oneself, mystical experience is not reserved to Christians. It is a universal phenomenon to which all religions bear witness in diverse forms and at different degrees. I have therefore read the works of non-Christian mystics, to see if their experience bears out the Christian conception of God as One and Three. But I have found among them no direct, unambiguous testimony to Trinitarian doctrine. The mystics of world-religions, authentic as I do not doubt their experience often to be, have achieved or received

a supremely vivid inkling of some of the divine
attributes. They have grasped something of the
transcendence and the immanence of God. God as the
All-Other, as Brahman, has been sensed as intimately present within, as Atman. God as Ishvara
the supreme Lord, who calls and sends prophets,
has been obeyed and followed with profound fidelity. God as supreme Lover has been known and
loved to the utmost of human capacity in ineffable
interchanges which escape full description. God as
eternal has been glanced at in the timeless present into which some mystics have somehow already,
for a fleeting moment, been introduced. God as
tenderly attentive providence has been felt to
guide those who have surrendered to divine initiative. Even at times without being named, without
being touched or apprehended or imagined or attributed to a center of consciousness, there have
been sensed divine dimensions looming beyond all
affirmation and all negation. Affirmed as neither
existing nor non-existing, perceived as ultimate
Void, God has called disciples who have left all
things in total denudation.

The many and diverse mysticisms of non-Christian religions allow us to detect the truth expressed in those words spoken by Krishna in the
Bhagavad-Gita: "In any way that men have loved me,
in that same way they find my love: for many are
the paths of men, but they all in the end come to
me".3 Yet this is not what I seek when I seek for
the Three.

I have been inspired by the Chandogya-upanishad
and the Gita. I have glimpsed at some ineffable
breakthrough in reading about Zen-masters. Above
all, I have been edified by a humble Senegalese
Moslem, a member of the Tidjane confraternity,
talking about the "power" of Friday, the day of
Allah, and the "power" of Monday, the day of the
Prophet. To obtain a vivid experience of some of
the divine attributes is a high privilege which I
envy many non-Christian devotees. To have been
introduced to some yet unknown, yet unrevealed attribute of God,has transported some of them beyond

this world into a totally new and perhaps more real dimension of life. To enter somehow the depths of the divine nature, the pervasive character of the divine presence, the untold power of the divine action, is indeed a grace. Though undeserved by any creature, it has been graciously offered by God in the mysteries and the secrecies of divine Love, even outside of Christianity, even outside of the religions of the Book. But this is not yet the experience of the Three.

Christian mystics too have entered the realms described by non-Christians. With Paul they have "longed to be freed from this life" (Phil., 1:23); they have "grasped the breadth and length and height and depth" of Christ's love, and experienced "this love which surpasses all knowledge" (Eph., 3:18). They have been raised, like Augustine during the vision of Ostia, through material creation, through the self, to a touch of Eternal Wisdom.[4] They have plunged into the divine attributes, described by John of the Cross in stanzas 14 and 15 of the Spiritual Canticle (version B):

> My Beloved - oh, mountains,
> lovely wooded valleys,
> strange islands,
> tingling creeks,
> whistle of air in love,
> tranquil night
> at the moment of the rising dawn,
> silent music,
> echoing solitude,
> refreshing, enamoring supper...

Through their experience of God, Christian mystics have acquired a self-knowledge incomprehensible to others. Who can fathom the humility of Angela da Foligno, asserting: "I see myself along with God, all pure, all holy, all truth, all righteousness, all secure, all heavenly in him"?[5] With Dionysius, Christian mystics have advanced "beyond all sensation and all intellection and all objects whether sensed or seen and all being and all nonbeing...", thus being led "in utter pureness, rejecting all and released from all, aloft to the flashing forth, beyond all being, of the divine dark."[6]   Yet in the divine dark they have perceived a unity with God that can only be expressed paradoxically. Meister Eckhart wrote: "In bursting forth I discover that God and I are One."[7]   With Symeon the New Theologian and the monks of Mount Athos, Christian mystics have seen the divine light.   Being transfigured by the light of Mount Tabor, as Gregory Palamas explained it, they have lived entirely in God, and God in them.[8] Indeed, there is no mystical experience of the world-religions - positive or negative, of immanence or transcendence, of fulness or of void - but has its parallel among Christian mystics. But this is not yet the experience of the Three.

I am aware of course that the study of comparative religion has detected various adumbrations of Trinitarian doctrine outside of Christianity.   There are Platonic trilogies in the Timaeus (such as, fire, earth, water-air); and Carl Jung has drawn attention to the symbolic question asked at the beginning of the Timaeus: "One, two, three - where is the fourth...?"[9] There is a neo-Platonic trilogy (the One, the Nous, the Soul). There are Hindu trilogies (Brahma, Vishnu, Krishna at the level of divine names, Brahman, Ishvara, advaita, at the level of experiential participation in the divine).   There is the Mahayana doctrine of the three bodies of the Buddha. There are the Valentinian conception of divine emanations and the Kabbalist contemplation of the ten sephirot.   But is this the experience of the Three?

Rather than attempt the impossible task of deciphering the Three Persons of the Christian faith in these and other religious myths, I have myself classified the religions of the world into two main groups.[10] Religions of the Spirit have been sensitive to the universal divine presence and action, finding God or divine traces or sparks of divinity in everything that is, identifying the divine as the permanent stuff of the universe beyond all passing appearances and phenomena. Religions of the Father, sensing the fatherhood and the motherhood of God as creator and providence, as life-giving and nurturing, have identified God as one or several transcendent Persons benevolently inclined toward their devotees. But this is not yet an experience of the Three.

o

Initiation into the triune life of God dominates the spiritual experience of Christians. All the great mystics of the Christian tradition witness to this. The ascent to God is a progress in the tri-une life, a march, like that of Moses through the desert, toward and into what has been described symbolically as the summit of a mountain or the depths of a cave. The living God, revealed through the Word made flesh, understood in the Spirit, is identified as the Three whom our imperfect language calls Father, Son, Spirit. In the oneness between God and the human soul the mystics have perceived more than oneness, saying with Meister Eckhart:

> ...there is an agent in the soul, untouched by time and flesh, which proceeds out of the Spirit and which remains forever in the spirit and completely spiritual. In this agent, God is perpetually verdant and flowering with all the joy and glory that is in him. Here is joy so hearty, such inconceivably great joy that no one can ever fully tell it, for in this agent the eternal Father is ceaselessly begetting his eternal Son and the agent is parturient with God's Offspring and is itself the Son, by the Father's unique power.[11]

Specifically, the inner life of Christian mystics hinges on becoming one with the incarnate Word who, associating the faithful to his eternal filiation, brings them into his relationships with the Spirit and with the Father. By faith through

98

grace the disciples are one with Jesus. Knowing Jesus as their savior, a man delegated by God for their redemption, they learn to know him also as the eternal Word. His sayings pronounced on earth and recorded in Scripture nourish the Church's memory, enabling its members to go forth in hope toward greater oneness with the Only-begotten, the eternally spoken divine Word. The actions of the incarnate Word on earth lead to what the Word does now in the Spirit, opening for us the literally infinite perspective of the uncreated Word through whom the Father reveals himself to himself in the Spirit from everlasting to everlasting. The immanent Trinity, at work in the words and deeds of Jesus the Christ, comes to be experienced and somehow, up to a point, imperfectly, understood as transcendent Trinity. The flesh of Jesus has been the epiphany of the tri-une Divinity. Thus one may distinguish some basic steps of the mystical ascent: first, an assimilation of the disciples to Jesus Christ as he lived in Palestine; second, an ascent from Jesus known according to the flesh to Jesus known according to the Spirit; third, a flowering of the inner life into the relations of the eternal Word with the Spirit and with the Father.

Yet this need not be a neat sequence of events rigidly followed. On the contrary, Christian mysticism is as varied as it is deep; and I cannot even begin to suggest either its variety or its depth in the few pages of this chapter. Yet, lest silence be interpreted as dissent, I will briefly listen to some of the Christian mystics as they report on their ascent to God.

o

Until well into the twentieth century, the Imitation of Christ served to initiate many Christians, Protestant no less than Catholic, to the life of inner discipleship. Jean-Martin Moye (1730-1793) represented a broad consensus of the spiritual tradition when he wrote: "Read this book

99

carefully: you will find everything in it".[12] Before the Imitation was written in the fifteenth century, other books rendered similar services, notably the Meditationes de vita Christi. Before these, a simple lectio divina or meditative reading of the Scriptures, modeled on the commentaries of Gregory the Great, performed the same task. Periodically, revival movements drew attention to the humanity of Jesus and its importance for the spiritual life. So did St Bernard and the Cistercians in the twelfth century, the Franciscans in the thirteenth, the devotio moderna in the fifteenth, Ignatius Loyola, with his Exercises, in the sixteenth. In each case, the humanity of Jesus served as the starting point and the ladder of ascent toward the divinity of Christ and the Three Persons.

The narrow focus is no less clear than the broad picture. Because mystical experience should not primarily be a matter for historical study in writings of long ago, I have looked at the testimony of the recently famous, yet now largely neglected Thérèse of the Child Jesus (1873-1897). As Thérèse describes her childhood in the towns of Alençon and Lisieux, she must have been an unbearable child, pious and sweet no doubt, but so sensitive as to force her loving family to treat her with infinite reserve and delicacy, making her, who was the "baby", the youngest, into the "little queen" of their middle-class household and especially of her father. Throughout her short life, her conventional versification, which was notably devoid of poetry, kept a tinge, and more than a tinge, of sugary sentimentality. At the same time a strain of masochism, which may have been a defense mechanism triggered by her frequent pains and aches, affected her piety. Her insistence, at fifteen years of age, that she wanted to join the Carmel before the canonical age, and her personal appeal to Pope Leo XIII exhibit the features of an ego-trip. But none of this can detract from what Thérèse did become in her spiritual journey.

She considered the years 1877, following her

mother's death, to 1886 as the "winter" of her life. During a sickness she was oriented toward a spiritual vocation by what she took to be a vision of the Virgin Mary, smiling at her and healing her (May 13, 1883). At Christmas 1886, at 13 years of age, a grace of inner transformation launched her on the mystic way. "On this luminous night" she writes, "which enlightens the lights of the Holy Trinity, Jesus, the sweet little child of one hour, changed the night of my soul by a flood of light." [13] Thérèse finds herself transformed, made "strong and courageous." From then on, she was "not vanquished in any struggle, but on the contrary marched from victory to victory and began, as it were, a giant's race." This "complete conversion" is accompanied by a christocentric insight: "In one instant, the task that I had not been able to do in ten years was accomplished by Jesus, who accepted the good will which I never lacked...Jesus himself took the net, threw it, and brought it back filled with fish...He made me a fisher of souls... In a word, I felt charity enter my heart, the need to forget myself in order to please others; and from that time on I was happy." [14] Thérèse relates to Jesus in a new way and more vividly than before: "The cry of Jesus on the cross resounded continually in my heart: I thirst. These words kindled in me an unknown, most vivid zeal...I wanted to give something to drink to my Beloved and I felt myself devoured by a thirst for souls..."

After this moment, Thérèse passes speedily through stages which, in others, may take many years. Her entering the Carmel at seventeen in 1888 is remarkable enough, but her inner growth is still more amazing. As a Carmelite she feels great peace at first, but she slowly enters a cloud of dryness and of temptations against faith, where she experiences "great interior tests of all kinds (going as far as wondering at times if heaven exists)." [15] She finds little or no consolation in prayer, is unable to meditate, struggles through the rosary. She is occasionally sustained by new insights. Yet she has a dogged determination to be faithful to Jesus and to her calling. As assistant to the novice-mistress she shows great maturity and a spiritual insight that can derive only from experience. In 1895, on the Sunday of the Trinity, a Trinitarian breakthrough pierces her. Admittedly, she does not describe it directly as being Trinitarian. Yet the accent is unmistakable. What she discovers on that day is the "infinite Love" manifested in Jesus. But love, italicized (Amour) or capitalized (AMOUR), is more than a feeling or an attitude. "Ah, since that happy day it has seemed to me that Love penetrates and surrounds me, that at every moment this Merciful Love renovates me, purifies my soul and leaves in it no trace of sin..."[16] Love is a person; it is the Holy Spirit of the Christian tradition. Under the impact of this discovery, Thérèse composes an "act of self-offering to Merciful Love." This is addressed to "the Blessed Trinity" and at the same time to God the Father who has given her his only Son as her savior and spouse. The Spirit is not named; but it is the Spirit whom Thérèse calls "the divine Look,"[17] who takes the form of Merciful Love, to whom she offers herself "as a holocaust victim to YOUR MERCIFUL LOVE."[18] Nothing is more revealing than Thérèse's short writing addressed to her eldest sister Marie, Sister Mary of the Blessed Sacrament. Jesus, she explains, teaches her "in secret," and not through consolations and in books. Yet she is learning "the science of LOVE," aware that the Spirit in Scripture promised himself to little ones. The Spirit is "the essential Painter who alone will be able, after the night of this life, to provide me with the colors able to paint the marvels which he unveils before the eye of my soul."[19] She reports her dream vision of Anne of Jesus, the companion of St Teresa of Avila, who introduced the Carmel into France. This dream confirmed her in her self-offering to divine Love. She understands that Love is at the center of all: "MY VOCATION IS LOVE. Yes, I have found my place in the Church, and this place, o my God, you gave me yourself...in the Heart of the Church my Mother, I will be Love...thus I will be all..."[20] And then, echoing St John of the Cross,

102

she addresses herself to Love: "O luminous Light of love, I know how to reach you, I have found the secret of how to appropriate your flame." As Elisha begged Elijah for "HIS TWOFOLD SPIRIT" (2 Kings 2: 9), that is, for a double portion of his spirit, so she begs all the inhabitants of heaven for the gift of their "TWOFOLD LOVE."[21] Being now set by Love at the very center of all, she discovers the universality of her vocation. She feels "the calling of WARRIOR, of PRIEST, of APOSTLE, of DOCTOR, of MARTYR."[22] Would she were all the saints at once! But she knows that "LOVE contains all callings, that love is all, that it embraces all times and all places...in a word, that it is eternal!..." Shortly before dying, on September 30, 1896, she sums up her way in these words: "I do not regret giving myself up to Love. Oh, no, I do not regret it, on the contrary."[23]

Thérèse's perception of God the Father is deeply rooted in her empathetic participation in the tragedy which struck her own father shortly after her admission to the Carmel. From February 12,1889 to his death on July 29,1894, her father had to be institutionalized, his cerebral functions being affected by hardening of the arteries. He sank into a night, of which Thérèse, still a child (in 1879 or 80), had had a preview in a sort of waking vision: she thought she saw him wandering outside the house with his face veiled. After he had entered this hidden life, behind a veil, as it were, Thérèse asked for her additional name. Thérèse "of the Child Jesus" became "and of the Holy Face." Whose Face was this? Her own self-offering to Merciful Love aspires to the moment when she may "tell her Love" to her Beloved in "an Eternal Face to Face."[24] Christ's Face, suffering and triumphant, reflects the Father's hidden Face. The divine Word is "the Eagle contemplated at the center of the Sun of Love"...drawing us "to the Eternal Hearth of the Blessed Trinity"...returning "to the inaccessible Light..."[25] The Hidden Face is that of the Father. And so Thérèse, while she feels deeply her human father's trial, is at peace. "The good God" is "the Thief" of whom she speaks

103

in the last months of her life,[26] who will soon snatch her away too. But he also is "Papa le bon Dieu,"[27] "Daddy the good God," the eternal Father, who is not far from us even when he remains hidden. On the one hand, Thérèse asserts: "I understand and I know by experience that the kingdom of God is within us."[28] On the other, she states during her final illness: "I no longer want the wine of the earth...I want to drink of the new wine in my Father's kingdom."[29] The Father is both near and far; he is Light and Sun, yet veiled. We now are on pilgrimage to his kingdom. Jesus, the Beloved, leads us to the Father through the Fire of Love, which is the Holy Spirit.

o o o

The Trinitarian perceptions of the mystics can be abundantly illustrated. A few cursory instances will suffice. Claudine Moine (1618-d. after 1655), the "mystic seamstress of Paris," is primarily a mystic of Christ and of the eucharistic presence. But the mysteries of Christ lead her to the divine being, to the attributes of God, and finally to the Three Persons. She writes: "One day, on the eve or the feast of the Holy Trinity, I obtained a great and extraordinary light, and most unexpectedly."[30] There follows a description of this light along the lines of the conventional Trinitarian theology which Claudine may have heard in sermons or read in books. But one senses the ring of existential truth in the ensuing statement: "For about two years henceforth I had as it were a continual view of this adorable mystery. My soul was always in the presence of the most holy Trinity, unceasingly seeing how the Father begets his Son, and the Father and the Son together produce the Holy Spirit, this being the eternal occupation of God: to know himself and to love himself...I had a special devotion to this great and profound mystery..."[31] Claudine wrote at the time a short treatise on the Trinity, which she unfortunately burnt on the advice of a priest.

Mary of the Incarnation (1599-1672), the Ursuline of Quebec, is chiefly a mystic of the divine Word, the heart of her experience residing in a passage from Jesus known according to the flesh, in his humanity, to Jesus known according to the Spirit, in the divinity of the Word. What she calls her sixth stage of prayer includes a close union with the Three Persons. She is then about twenty-six years old, a widow with a little son. The following page is remarkable both for its theological accuracy and for its spiritual acumen:

....in one moment my eyes were closed and my spirit was raised and absorbed in the sight of the most holy and august Trinity in a manner that I cannot express. In that moment, all the faculties of my soul were halted and they received the impression that was given them of this sacred mystery. This impression was without form or shape, more clear and intelligible than any light. It made me know that my soul was in the truth, which, in a moment, made me see the divine exchange that the three divine Persons have together; the Father's love, who, contemplating himself, begets his Son, which has been from all eternity and will be eternally; my soul was informed by this truth in an ineffable manner which makes me lose all words; it was drowned in this light. Then it understood the mutual love of the Father and the Son producing the Holy Spirit, which took place through a mutual plunge of love without mingling or confusion. I received the impression of this production, understanding spiration and production... Seeing the distinctions, I knew the unity of essence among the three divine Persons; and although I need several words to say it, it was in one moment, without any time sequence, that I knew the unity, the distinctions, and the operations in themselves and outside of themselves. Yet in a way I was progressively enlightened, in keeping with the operations of the three divine Persons in themselves, finding no mingling in each knowledge of the things that were given me to understand, all this with unexpressible purity and clarity.[32]

This experience lasted "the time of several masses", something like a couple of hours. But the impression remained. For a long time Mary experienced the Trinity within, whatever else she was doing externally. Her remaining stages of prayer (she numbers thirteen of them) brought about a progressive deepening of this Trinitarian experience. She saw herself within each of the Three Persons, participating in its divine life. The ninth stage universalized her vocation: she saw herself in all countries where the gospel still needed to be proclaimed, and she felt destined to the "country of the Hurons," that is, Quebec, where she landed in 1639. Her thirteenth stage, the most ineffable, is a "very high and very pure union." She then feels "quite an extraordinary clarity in the ways of the superadorable Spirit of the incarnate Word, whom I experience in great purity and certainty as being objective Love, intimately united and uniting my spirit to his own, and [I experience] that all he has said has spirit and life in me."[33] Her soul has "life only in him [the incarnate Word], in this basic state of love, night and day, at every moment."[34]

o o o

Turning to John of the Cross's poem, The Spiritual Canticle, I am struck, not only by the beauty of the poem and the theological depth of the commentary, but also and primarily by the very structure of the project.[35] It is not because the author paraphrases Trinitarian doctrine poetically: this he does more thoroughly in Romances 1 and 2. Nor is it because he describes a Trinitarian experience: this is done in all his poetry and the accompanying commentaries. The Dark Night effectively depicts the horizon of Trinitarian experience, the night of faith, developing into the night of sense and of spirit. The Living Flame describes the high moment of this experience when, in spiritual marriage, love becomes inflamed, informed, by the Holy Spirit. What makes the Spiritual Canticle unique is that the poem no less than the poet is shaped by the perception of the Three. This is not a matter of poetic form or of the dialectic between the soul and the Beloved, which varies considerably, in the sequence of episodes, between the two versions of the poem. In order to explain what I mean, I will draw on Hjelmslev's glossematic.

One may distinguish between what Hjelmslev calls the level of expression and the level of content.[36] The two are related, the content emerging in the expression and nowhere else. But the content has no independent existence. It does not pre-exist to the poetic expression. John of the Cross did not dispose of a previous experience stored up in his memory, to which he would have given expression when he found time. In the case of this poem, time was provided for most of it against his will: the first thirty stanzas of redaction A were composed and memorized in gaol, from December 1577 to August 1578. But so was the content: the emergence of the content coincides in time and place with that of the expression. In the nomenclature of Hjelmslev, I would say that the form of the expression of the Cantico Espiritual (forty stanzas of five verses of the kind known in Spanish as the lira, a form of verse imported from Italy and popularized in Spain by Garcilaso de la Vega)[37] conveys the substance of the expression of the poem (the poetic experience, or, more precisely, the creative experience of writing). This in turn is inseparable from the form and substance of the content of the poem. The form of the content is the mystical experience of John of the Cross being raised to spiritual marriage in his Toledo gaol. The substance of the content is the Trinity itself as then experienced

107

by the mystic poet.

John of the Cross confirms this when he states unequivocally that the poem was inspired:

> These stanzas...were obviously composed with a certain burning love of God...Since these stanzas, then, were composed in a love flowing from abundant mystical under-standing, I cannot explain them ade-quately...[38]

The content of the poem is mystical theology, which, as John of the Cross explains, "is known through love and by [which] one not only knows but at the same time experiences." Thus the poem as such is mystical. It gives form to a poetic ex-perience, which is itself the outward shape of a mystical experience. And this mystical experi-ence is the form taken in John of the Cross by the communication of the Three Persons.

If we now focus on the form of the content of the poem, a structure appears immediately. One may distinguish a horizon and a series of successive interlocking foci.[39] The horizon, which provides the background and stands behind everything that takes place and every word that is said, is con-stituted by an intimate, all-pervading presence of the Beloved with the bride. The bride being the soul (here, John the Cross, but also, insofar as we, the readers, enter the intent of the poem, then we ourselves), the Beloved is the Word of God. The bride begins by searching for the Beloved, among shepherds, in the countryside, interrogating all creatures (st. 1-11). As she seeks, she dis-covers the Beloved, who lets himself be known in his works (st. 5-7) before contacting the bride directly (st. 8-13). As she feels carried away by the overwhelming experience of discovery, the Be-loved calls her back (st. 12-13), revealing some of his attributes and qualities (st. 14-19). The Beloved introduces her to spiritual marriage (st. 20-24) when she has been suitably prepared. The bride describes this marriage and expresses her desire for total and eternal union in heaven (st. 24-33). But the Beloved reminds her that life here is not ended and that she still lives and will live, in the solitude and happiness of the wound of love (st. 34-35). The last stanzas (36-40) contain a final song of love for the Beloved, in which the bride, as she is becoming the very beauty of the Beloved, already experiences total peace.

On this background of union with the divine Word, several foci are easily distinguishable. For the Beloved is not perceived always in the same manner. I find three foci, or, if one wills, three ways in which the Beloved is present in the soul that loves him.

There is presence in absence. The bride seeks for the Beloved because he is not here. Yet the words addressed to Pascal can apply: "You would not seek me unless you had found me."[40] When John of the Cross asks: Adonde te acondiste,/Amado, y me dejaste con gemido?[41] (Where have you hidden,/Beloved, and left me with my complaint?) he already suggests an answer: the Beloved is in the complaint, in the desire, in the "wound" of verse 4, in the "call" of verse 5: "You have fled like a hart/having left me wounded;/I went out after you, calling, but You were gone." Above all, the Beloved is in his own fleeing: he is gone; yet his flight, his absence, is perceived as his, and thereby as a positive event. The lover who is aware of the Beloved's absence is not abandoned. Absence is the negative side of presence. It is a presence in reverse. So John of the Cross the commentator explains the insight of the poet: "It should be known that the Word, the Son of God, together with the Father and the Holy Spirit, is hidden, in essence and in presence, in the innermost being of the soul" (st. 1, n.6).[42]

A second focus is presence in presence. "To the one who knocks it will be opened" (Luke 11:10). The Beloved's absence is not permanent. Creatures, when they are interrogated, testify about the Be-

109

loved: they have been marked by "who He is" (st. 5, n.1).[43] God - that is, the Father, has - through his Wisdom, the Word, left his traces in all creation, an "I-know-not-what" which all things mumble" (st. 7, n.9).[44] This general, vague, though positive, presence of the Beloved prepares the soul for his direct presence: he is light of her eyes, sight and beauty, presence and image. The soul enters the spiritual betrothals. The bride now is directly "touched" by her Beloved, deeply yet intermittently. She suffers from the limitations imposed on her joy by the Beloved's ebb and flow, by the alternance of touch and removal, of presence in presence and presence in absence. But she rejoices as she discovers the qualities, the adornments, the beauties, of the Beloved. In particular, she discerns, in the Word and as belonging to him, the divine attributes:

Mi Amado, las montañas,	My Beloved - oh, mountains,
Los valles solitarios nemorosos,	isolated wooded valleys,
Las insulas extranas,	strange islands,
Los rios sonorosos,	tingling creeks,
El silbo de los aires amorosos...[45]	whistle of breezes in love...

This leads to the deeper, more permanent, union of spiritual marriage, when "the bride has entered/the sweet longed-for garden/and rests in delight/her neck reclining/on the gentle arm of the Beloved"[46] (st. 22).

A third focus of the Beloved's presence is his speaking. The Word is heard. The Beloved speaks to the bride, calling her back (Vuelvete, paloma - Return, my dove...), silencing the lower parts of her soul (st. 20-23), describing her beauties and proclaiming his joy in her (st. 34-35). The bride need not now guess that the Beloved is near, she no longer needs to seek. She knows, by the evidence of her spiritual senses, that she has become hearer, in his words, of the Word. These are what the Ascent of Mount Carmel describes as "substantial locutions," by which the divine Speaker, as he addresses the soul, transforms her, effecting in her what his words say.[47]

Thus the Spiritual Canticle is and reports the experience of the divine Word by the soul. This horizon is illuminated by additional foci relating to the Spirit and to the Father. For the Word whom the soul seeks, to whom she is engaged and then joined in marriage, makes her share, with some of the attributes of his divine nature, his intradivine relationships.

The Beloved introduces the Spirit when he calls himself a "wounded hart/who appears on the hill/in the wind of your flight/and feels refreshed". John of the Cross comments: "He very appropriately terms this love which is caused by the flight air, because the Holy Spirit, who is Love, is also compared to air in Scripture, for the Holy Spirit is the breath of the Father and the Son...Just as love is the union of the Father and the Son, so is it the union of the soul with God"[48] (st. 13, n. 11). In the Spirit, in the divine spiration from the Father and the Son, the soul is enabled to reach the height of contemplation. In response, the soul, in stanza 17, desires and asks for the experience of divine spiration in herself: "South wind, come, you who bring to mind our loves,/ Breathe through my garden..."[49] Thus the Holy Spirit, who is "air of the flight", "invading torrent" (st. 14,n.9), "south wind", "fragrant amber" (st. 18, n.6), is communicated to the soul in successive touches until, being made "deiform and God by participation"[50] (st. 39, n.4) she shares in the spiration of the Spirit:"Even that which comes to pass in the communication given in this temporal transformation is unspeakable, for the soul united and transformed in God breathes out in God to God the very divine spiration which God – she being transformed in him – breathes out in himself to her" (st. 39, n.3).

God the Father also is present to the soul as another, or rather, as the ultimate focus of her experience of God. But it is characteristic of the First Person that, communicating only through the Son and in the Spirit, he remains in himself hidden. Indeed, it is in the Father that the Beloved is hidden when the soul searches for him (st. 1, n.3). So is the Father invoked by the soul in his presenceful absence: "Show me where you pasture and where you rest at midday" (Song of Songs, 1:6). This biblical verse is appropriated by John of the Cross, who comments: "The Son is the only delight of the Father, who rests nowhere else nor is present in any other than in his beloved Son"[51] (st. 1, n.5). So the soul knows that where the Son is, there is the Father and vice versa. Her search for the Beloved is by the same token a search for the hidden and Son-hiding Father. Yet, while hidden and at times hiding the Son, the Father communicates with us through his Image, which is no other than the Son: "With this image of his Son alone, he clothed them [the creatures] in beauty..."[52] (st. 5, n.4). And as not the Son only, but the Three Persons are hidden in the soul "in essence and in presence"[53] (st. 1, n. 6), the spiritual marriage entails a participation also in the Father in anticipation of fuller participation in heaven on "the other day"[54] of God's eternity (st. 38, n.5-6): "There would not be a true and total transformation if the soul were not transformed in the Three Persons of the Most Holy Trinity in an open and manifest degree"[55] (st. 39, n.3).

Admittedly, the last five stanzas of the Canticle were not composed in the spiritual flame of the Toledo prison. They were added later, most probably at Beas in Andalusia when John of the Cross commented on parts of the Ascent of Mount Carmel and of the Spiritual Canticle before the Carmelite sisters, some time between 1578 and 1581. More directly than the immediate experience, they express the mystical theologian's subsequent reflection about it. But John of the Cross, theologian, is the same person as John of the Cross, mystic and poet. His theology interprets the poetry and the experience out of which it arises. What has taken place he now understands as antici-

pating our eternal share of the divine beauty, and
he sings, in the immortal poetry of stanza 36:
Gocemonos, Amado,/y vamonos a ver en tu hermo-
sura...[56] (Let us rejoice, Beloved,/and let us go
and see each other in your beauty...).

o o o

If one takes these testimonies of the mystics
together, an overall pattern emerges. It is on the
background of a general, vague, undetermined apprehension of God as inner presence that non-
Christian mystics perceive from time to time some
of the attributes of God and become receivers of
divine gifts of discernment and action. It is likewise on the background of a general, vague, undetermined sense of the divine presence in them
that Christian mystics perceive,from time to time,
the word as the Mediator leading them, through a
deeper insight into the divine attributes, to the
Spirit as the strength which enables them to become more like God, and finally to the Father himself as present within and reached through what
the Word and the Spirit do at the center of their
being.   Thus the pattern of mystical experience
starts with a general, vague, undetermined presence of God, continues through some of the attributes of God implied in this inner presence, goes
on, at least for Christians, with a perception of
the mediating Word, through whom the general presence of God and the divine attributes are illuminated and deepened, is again specified as perception of the Third Person enabling us and strength-
ening us in love, in order finally to end with an
at least indirect perception of the Father.   All
this takes place through the alternances and simul-
taneities of light and of night by which the
mystic way is infinitely diversified.

Thus our own reflection about this experience
leads us to deepen our vision of the Three Persons.
It is now in the perspective of personal discovery
within our interior universe that we are invited
to see the Three.   The doctrine of the Trinity is

113

not primarily a teaching for the intellect to fathom and refine. Before all else, it should be the learning of a way: this is the path to as total a union with God as is possible in this life, in anticipation of the further union to be effected when each of us returns to our Father in heaven. "Do you not think," a spiritual author of the nineteenth century asks, "that our endeavor should be to go to God, through the knowledge of the Son, in the love of the Holy Spirit?"[57] This question sums up the entire contemplative tradition of Christianity. At the same time, it provides us with a further image of the Three. For this is once more the Trinitarian image of the gospels, though in reversed form. At the Jordan river we may know Jesus as the Beloved Son, the one who comes from the Father, on whom the Spirit rests in love; and as we become one with him in our knowledge of him, we ourselves also become beloved sons and daughters, on whom the Spirit rests, called to the beyond of the invisible Father, whose Image is within us as the incarnate Lord in the Spirit.

Perhaps at this point do we feel some nostalgia for an experience which we have not obtained. Perhaps do we consider that the mystic way, with its required self-discipline and its periods of dryness and its nights, is more to be admired than followed. And yet, my reader, if you or I have missed something of what has been offered to us, if somehow we are not aware of the fulfilment in us of the promise: "If someone loves me, he will keep my word, and my Father will love him; we will come to him, and make our dwelling with him" (J., 14:23) - is it not because somewhere along the way we have misread a signpost, we have not heard a small still voice calling to us, we have missed a turn?

But as one can never go back, one should now listen again more carefully, be more attentive, place oneself, as the modern mystic Simone Weil expressed it, en hypomone, "in patience," "in a state of watching, of waiting, of attention, of desire."[58]

114

1. See the distinction made by John Henry Newman: An Essay in Aid of a Grammar of Assent, ch. 4, New York, 1955, p. 48-92.

2. On the Trinitarian form of liturgical prayer, see George Every: Basic Liturgy, London, 1961. On the Trinitarian form of prayer in general, see Meditation on the Word, New York, 1968, p. 129-69; The Inner Life, New York, 1976, p. 90-94.

3. Juan Mascaro, tr.: The Bhagavad Gita, Baltimore, 1962, p. 62.

4. St Augustine: Confessions, bk IX, ch. 10, in Augustine: Confessions and Enchiridion (Library of Christian Classics), Philadelphia, n.d., p. 192-94.

5. Angela da Foligno: L'Esperienza di Dio Amore, Rome, 1972, p. 161.

6. Quoted in Elmer O'Brien: Varieties of Mystic Experience, New York, 1965, p. 69-70.

7. Meister Eckart: Sermon 28, in Raymond Blackney, tr.: Meister Eckhart, New York, 1957, p. 232.

8. On Symeon, see the introduction to his catecheses, by Basil Krivocheine (S. Chr., 96, Paris, 1963); on Palamas, see Jean Meyendorff: Byzantine Hesychasm: historical, theological and social problems, London, 1974; St.Gregory Palamas and Orthodox Spirituality, Crestwood, N.Y., 1974; A Study of Gregory Palamas, London, 1964.

9. Carl Jung, op. cit., p. 121-22; Plato: Timaeus, in Benjamin Jowett, tr.: The Dialogues of Plato, vol. 3, London, 1970, p. 196 ff.

10. See above, p. 57.

11. Op. cit., p. 209.

12. Georges Tavard: L'Expérience de Jean-Martin Moye, Paris, 1978, p. 93.

13. Thérèse de l'Enfant Jésus: Manuscrits Autobiographiques, Lisieux, 1957, p. 107.

14. op. cit., p. 109.

15. op. cit., p. 201.

16. op. cit., p. 211.

17. op. cit., p. 319.

18. op. cit., p. 320.

19. op. cit., p. 220.

20. op. cit., p. 229.

21. op. cit., p. 230-31.

22. op. cit., p. 229.

23. J'Entre dans la Vie. Derniers entretiens, Paris, 1973, p. 185.

24. Manuscrits autobiographiques, p. 320.

25. op. cit., p. 236.

26. J'Entre dans la Vie, p. 55, 67, 68...

27. op. cit., p. 41.

28. Manuscrits autobiographiques, p. 208.

29. J'Entre dans la Vie, p. 74.

30. Claudine Moine: Ma Vie Secrète, Paris, 1968, p. 350; see Jean Guennou: La Couturière Mystique de Paris, Paris, 1959.

31. op. cit., p. 351.

32. Marie de l'Incarnation: Autobiographie. Relation de 1654, Solesmes, 1976, p. 53-4.

33. op. cit., p. 130.

34. op. cit., p. 132.

35. My quotations will be taken from Kieran Kavanaugh and Otilio Rodriguez, tr.: The Collected
Works of St John of the Cross, Washington, 1973,
though I will occasionally depart from it for the
translation of the poetry. On John of the Cross,
see Georges Morel: Le Sens de l'existence selon S.
Jean de la Croix, 3 vol., Paris, 1960-61, and Hans
Urs von Balthasar's study of the poems in Herrlich-
keit, vol. II, Einsiedeln, 1962. Some scholars
have questioned the authenticity of the longer
version of the Spiritual Canticle and its commentary (usually designated as version B). I hold
that the two versions are authentic, B being the
author's enlargement of A. See the discussion in
Vida y Obras de San Juan de la Cruz (Biblioteca de
Auctores Cristianos), 2nd ed., Madrid, 1950, p.
924-51. My quotations will be from version B.

36. Louis Hjelmslev: Prolegomena to a Theory of
Language, Baltimore, 1953, ch. 13.

37. See Damaso Alonso: La Poesia de san Juan de la
Cruz, Madrid, 1958; Gerald Brennan: St John of
the Cross. His Life and Poetry, Cambridge (En-
gland), 1973.

38. Spiritual Canticle, prologue,1-3, in Collected
Works, p. 408-9.

39. On horizon and focus in theological writing,
see La Théologie parmi les sciences humaines,Paris,
1975, p. 36-9.

40. Jacques Chevalier, ed.: Pascal, Oeuvres com-
plètes, Paris, 1954, p. 1313.

41. Collected Works, p. 410.

42. op. cit., p. 418.

43. op. cit., p. 434.

44. op. cit., p. 440.

45. op. cit., p. 412.

46. op. cit., p. 413.

47. Ascent of Mount Carmel, bk II, ch. 31, in Collected Works, p. 210-211.

48. Collected Works, p. 461.

49. op. cit., p. 412.

50. op. cit., p. 558.

51. op. cit., p. 418.

52. op. cit., p. 435.

53. op. cit., p. 418.

54. op. cit., p. 555.

55. op. cit., p. 558.

56. op. cit., p. 546.

57. Emmanuel d'Alzon (1810-1880): Ecrits spirituels, Rome, 1956, p. 217.

58. Simone Weil: La Connaissance surnaturelle, Paris, 1950, p. 208; Pensées sans ordre concernant l'amour de Dieu, Paris, 1962, p. 144. "The state of waiting which is thus rewarded (in Luke 12:35-7) is what is commonly called patience. But the Greek word, hypomone, is infinitely more beautiful and carries another meaning. It designates a man who waits without moving, in spite of all the blows with which one tries to make him move: karpophorousin en hypomone - they will bear fruit in patience (Luke, 8:15)" (op. cit., p. 145).

V

The Discourse

The oldest and so far the most fruitful approach to the Trinitarian experience and conceptualization of God has been from the Johannine analogy of the Word. The notion of word opens the perspective of both inner and outer self-communication; it gives plausibility to the psychological theory; when related to the Johannine conception of God as love, it shows up the possibility of further analogies based on the analysis of love, whether in their Augustinian form, Amans, amatum, amor, or in their Ricardian form, Dilector, dilectus, condilectus. Yet, however enlightening such lines of thought have been, contemporary research into language may lead still further, toward understanding and personally assimilating Trinitarian doctrine and experience. The advances of the last half-century in linguistic science place the present time in a good position to appreciate the revelation of the Word of God, and to develop doctrine and experience on the fundamental Christian revelation of God as Three. The stakes are high. For if Trinitarian doctrine in the strict sense is proper to Christianity, the concept of a divine Word is not. Christians would not be acknowledging the Word of God unless the Hebrew prophets had on many occasions proclaimed a Dabar Adonai, a "word of the Lord", and unless the Jews of immediately pre-Christian times had identified Dabar, Word, as a suitable metaphor to designate God communicating his message. And this stress on the divine Word is not unique to Judaism. Islam is entirely grounded in the Koran as God's own word, which some schools have considered to be uncreated and some have even identified personally with the Prophet Mohammed. Even outside the "religions of the Book" the notion of divine Word is not unknown.[1]

o o o

Any one who looks up a Greek dictionary discovers that the Johannine term, Logos, which is at the heart of the Gospel of John, means speech, discourse, as well as word, term. Further denotations of Logos, referring to different parts of language or grammar, are variants on these basic meanings. Use of the same word to designate revelation or the reason behind a discourse belongs itself to the inner logic of meaningful discourse. Of these senses of the term, which are evidently interrelated, the theological tradition has chiefly retained three. It has reflected on the Second Person as God's eternally spoken one Word, which contains in itself both the ultimate reason of all things that are and the possibility of this ultimate reason being revealed through prophetic utterances. These theological meanings of logos have been linked, I would suggest, to the predominance of semantics over syntax in the popular or semi-popular concept of grammar with which Christian theologians have commonly functioned. Syntax itself, in pre-scientific linguistics, is only a way of putting words together, meaning being thus reduced to the combined sumtotal of the denotations of the words used when strung together in previously agreed fashion. As, by analogy with human words, the one Word of God is said to be conceived from God's mind, it may be called, analogically, God's Son. The idea of divine Fatherhood and Sonship is thus closely related to a pre-scientific understanding of word.

One need not reject the progress that the older approach to language and grammar allowed theology to make toward understanding the revelation of God as One and Three. Yet, by the same token, a more organic interpretation of logos should lead further into the theology of the Trinity.

Words, previously identified as the singular units, themselves made of one or more syllables, of which a sentence is made, have become very dubious in modern linguistics. At most, such words may be found in some extremely analytic languages, where they are more clearly recognizable when writing separates them on a page than when speech

120

merges them together in one flow. But they do not exist in agglutinating languages; and they are difficult to isolate, even when written, in languages with declensions and flexions. Instead of words one should speak of "units of meaning", which may comprise less or more than what the older approach identified as a word. When arranged together in a certain order identified as significant in a given language, a number of units of meaning constitute a discourse. From this one may gather that the Logos which introduced the Trinitarian conception into the notion of God is to be understood as divine Discourse rather than as the single component of a discourse. To translate Logos as Speech would be more correct than as Word. For there is no speech but spoken and no speech but expressive of meaning, whereas the old-fashioned word could well be unspoken, and could be spoken as an abracadabra with no recognizable sense. Logos as speech or discourse implies the structure of communication between those who speak and those who are spoken to. It brings in the communicative implications of the Johannine name for the Second Person. But these are in fact more elaborate than some recent authors have said.[2]

A human discourse (and we have no experience of any other kind) has two major characteristics, to which I will now draw attention. It is set in an external structure of communication; and it is itself internally structured.

Reduced to its simplest elements, the external structure of communication is threefold. It implies a speaker, an addressee, and a semiotic system functioning as a bridge between them. A semiotic system can be non-linguistic, being made, for instance, of looks, gestures, inarticulate sounds, conventional moving of pawns on a checkboard. But linguistic systems (as many systems as there are languages) are, in our experience, the most effective as well as the most elaborate semiotic systems and, presumably, the most effective because the most elaborate. With a finite set of units of meaning and a finite number of syntactic rules,

121

they allow us to generate an indefinite number of discourses. A linguistic system exists, for eventual speakers, as their permanent possibility for communicative discourse. This is la langue, language as a set of conventions with which to combine certain units of meaning so that the speaker's intent will be grasped. When the linguistic system is concretely put to use to convey definite ideas, we have la parole, a sample of spoken languages, a speech.

To say, with the gospel of John (rendered literally): "In the beginning was the Logos, and the Logos was with the God, and God was the Logos..." is to place within God the structure of communicative discourse: "In the beginning was Discourse, and Discourse was with God, and Discourse was divine..." In the context of the Johannine Gospel this refers to self-communication within God. And it is the basis for further communication with creation which is given its possibility in verse 3 ("All was made through it"), is described in its pre-Christian forms in verses 9 to 13 ("It was the true light that enlightens every man...it came among its own and its own received it not..."),and reaches its climax in verse 14: "And Discourse was made flesh..." There is Discourse of God to and with humankind because there is in the first place Discourse within God, Discourse from and to God. God is Speaker, and Addressee, and Discourse between them. Investing these terms with their Trinitarian equivalents, one may say that the Father expresses himself by way of the Word as his eternal Wisdom and Image. The Divinity, whose recondite, abysmal Urgrund is also Ungrund, becomes Expressed Expression. The Second Person is the Expression, emerging, as Ignatius of Antioch wrote, from the Silence of the Father. But discourse is always addressed; it has a direction. Expression is for the sake of impression. The first chapter of John does not make the Addressee clear. But the trend of the whole gospel points to the Spirit as the Addressee. The Spirit is the Impression, the Imprint coming to light as the divine Expression leaves its mark on, is received, is heard by, the

Divinity whence it comes. Thus God is not only, in the words of St Anselm, that than which nothing greater can be thought. God is also That than Which nothing greater can be Said. That denotes the Unoriginate, the first, the origin, the source of light, the speaker, the Father, who provides both the impetus to speak and the substance of what is spoken; Said indicates the Discourse, the Wisdom, the Word which is spoken and, as it is spoken, is expressive of all that the Source is; Which designates the Spirit, in whom the totality of Divinity is, as it is expressed, impressed, who is, both as teleology and as terminality, the end of the ways of God.

There is also an internal structure of communication, which itself is twofold as it may be considered from a syntactic or from a semantic point of view. Let us begin with syntax. Syntax provides the speakers of a language with ways to combine units of meaning in order to express and communicate signification. It is by their syntax that languages basically differ from one another, and by their syntactic similarities that the languages of the world can be classified in groups or families. At least theoretically, a language could preserve its syntax even if its vocabulary happened, through some extraordinary concourse of events, to be totally changed. In other words, syntax is both the characteristic, the most dynamic, and yet the most stable constituent of language. It is syntax which, in multifaceted applications, makes discourse expressive of all the values and riches intended by speakers. This should teach us at least, regarding divine Discourse, that the absolute simplicity of God - which Christian faith attributes equally to the Second Person as to the First and the Third, since all three are, singly and together, the totality of the divine substance - can be the source of an inexhaustible wealth of expression. The exemplaristic theologies of the past, which saw the Logos as the eternal model of all things that are, litted up a basic element of the theology of Discourse: the Discourse which is the Second Person is - in the absolute - unfathomable and inexhaustible.

Yet if no human analysis can ever hope to number and to measure the infinite actualities of divine Discourse, this provides no excuse from trying to discover, within the limits of analogy, which syntactic operation may characterize the Logos. Syntax works with a limited and recognizable set of rules, and there is no apriori reason why one could not discern which of our syntactic operations provides the most appropriate model for divine Discourse. Divine Discourse is essentially about the divine; it is theo-logy in the supreme sense of the expression. It is therefore among the operations of theological syntax that one should seek for such a model.

This assumes evidently that theology is itself a discourse, that there exists a theological language, and that the syntax of this language can be determined. There should be no need for me to enter into details at this point, as I have devoted an entire book to an investigation of theology as language.[3] Suffice it to say that, in researching the syntactic structure of theology as language, I have identified three basic orders of operations, which correspond to the three functions of comparison, participation, and proof. From the intentional principle of a theology, which expresses the correlation of horizon and focus in the theologian's intention, there flows an order of comparison, in which the diverse sceneries of a theological horizon are compared in the light of their focus. Participation follows upon the normative principle of a theology, by which sources of theological information are investigated and interpreted. It "designates the attempt to discover if and how a given reality brings about another, draws it out, determines it".[4] There are several modes of participation, which I have reduced to identification, typology, the spiritual senses, and analogy of faith. The order of proof has the function of constructing and testing the explanatory models of a theology. It proceeds by way of causality, rationality, and historiality.

This brief enumeration of the orders of theological operations sufficiently suggests which of them can serve as a model for understanding divine Discourse. There is nothing to compare to anything else in God, since comparison is between entities, distinct beings, and God is, for Christian theology no less than for the Islamic and Jewish faiths, supremely one in being. Models may indeed be applied to the concept of God and, whenever possible, they should be tested and verified. But this is due to the weakness of the human intellect. God needs no model of self to think about himself; nor does God need to prove anything to himself or to anyone else. Participation is the proper designation for the mutual relationships of the divine Persons and for their identity with the one divine substance or reality. The interrelationships of the Three were said by the Council of Florence to constitute "an opposition of relation".[5] The three Persons do not stand one to the others in a relation of opposition, by which each would, as it were, neutralize the others. They stand in the opposition of relation which is necessary for each to participate in the others. This relation is not negative – a contradiction; it is positive – a participation. The Son participates in the Father by receiving all that the Father is except that of the Father which is the Unoriginate; and this "that" is no other than the Father in his distinctiveness as Person. Said in another way, divine Discourse expresses, conveys, the totality of the divine substance expressing itself as the Source, as the Father. It participates, to the fullest extent of what participation can be, in the communicative intent of the Father as bonum diffusivum sui, the ultimate good which radiates its own goodness around. Divine Speech so fully participates in what it says that the divine Self-Expression is totally fulfilled in it. Or, to paraphrase the words of St. John of the Cross, "God has already told us all things in his Word, his Son, and he has no other word."[6] The Father, of course, does not participate, but is participated in. It is the Father's very substance which is shared through his self-diffusive radiation in Discourse.

125

The Spirit, as the recipient of divine Discourse, the interpreter of divine language, the decipherer of divine Script, participates in the fulness of the Father's substance, receiving it unrestrictedly as it is totally communicated in divine speech. From the First, through the Second, to the Third, the totality of divinity passes, in what the old theology called a circumincession or perichoresis. The Third is appropriately called Spirit, for it is characteristic of language that, as it is received, it is understood; the thought expressed, the reality conveyed, the discourse enunciated come to rest and fruition as spirit in the listener's mind. If one may at this point use the categories of J. L. Austin, divine Speech is supremely "performative".[7] What it says is not only said; it is also done, and done as and when said. The receiver of the Discourse is no foreign addressee: the divine Spirit is no other than the substance spoken by the Father in the Logos, as this substance comes to rest and fruition as divinely heard and received. The Third is the auditor and the audition, performed as the Second is spoken by the First, and performed in this very speaking.

Once the basic structure of language has provided a model for the theology of the Three Persons, the sophisticated uses of language in tale-telling or myth-making provide a further model.[8] Reduced to its simplest framework, a tale describes a first, primordial state of a hero or heroes, a series of more or less complex events through which this state is transformed, and a consequent or final state of the same hero or heroes resulting from these events. It thus has three terms, in which one can easily recognise an addressor, a message, an addressee; the past, the present, the future of historical sequences; the challenge, the trial, the victory of epics; the data of nature, their transformation by culture, the resulting access to higher civilization, which are at the core both of theories of social progress and of revolutionary strategy. Every experience, individual or collective, of telelogical nisus, of messianic expectation and hope, rests upon a similar structure.

Applied to the traditional Christian conception and experience of God, this structure well corresponds to the theology of the Trinity, as long as all hints of a time sequence have been carefully eliminated. This model applies to the doctrine of the Trinity ontologically, not chronologically. From the primodial depths of Divinity, called the Father, there emerges in the total instant of eternity an Event - the Word or Son - in which the Father expresses himself; and this movement of self-expression reaches its telos, its end, in being received by the self-same Divinity as what is called the Spirit. In this case also, the central Event, the speaking of the Word, the sending of the Message, is the key to Trinitarian doctrine. This heart of the Trinitarian vision makes it possible to project into knowing God the universal experience of humankind, which, as it advances in civilization, cannot resist the need to tell its stories, to compose its sagas, to sing its epics, to interpret its life as a passage from a primordial moment to an ultimate moment, as a transitus from an antecedent golden age lost in the rich pregnancy of the past to an eschatological restoration in a new heaven and a new earth. Such a passage, is as story, saga, epic, shaped and sung as a message. It serves as the transcendental model for story-tellers all the world over, from the Anglo Saxon scop to the West African griot of our day, from the holy stories of Prophets to the home-spun fairy tales of childhood. We are thus brought back to the inescapable centrality of the symbol of word, message, discourse, in the Christian revelation of God.

o o o

The syntactic dimension of language leads in turn to the semantic dimension. This refers to the identification and interpretation of the units of meaning of a given language. To simplify matters, we need not discuss here to what extent these

units of meaning correspond to the words or terms
of classical grammars; nor need we enter into problems of philology, etymology, or phonology. The
only question that should retain our attention
concerns the value which is attributed to a semantic unit when its meaning is recognized.   This
value and its components have been analyzed clearly
by Louis Hjelmslev and A. J. Greimas following the
impetus given to modern linguistics by Ferdinand
de Saussure.[9]

   Briefly, a unit of meaning denotes a conventional correspondence of a set of sounds to a
given object. When I hear the sounds /horse/, I
understand that a specific animal is referred to.
When I hear the sounds /cheval/, I also identify
the same animal.   Yet the sounds /horse/ and
/cheval/ have distinctive connotations, as when
the first is heard in the midst of a horse-loving
people like the English, just before a famous race
at Epsom Downs, or Princess Elizabeth rides her
horse in an international competition, and when
the second is heard by someone whose recent ances-
tors were small farmers who depended for their
livelihood on two or three solid work horses.
While some of these connotations belong to each
one's personal history and are of the order of
feelings, others can be objectified in a strictly
logical way. This is the purpose of the "quadrilateral of meaning", in which it is determined
that an object (S) is necessarily related to three
others: to its antithesis or contradiction (-S),
to that which differs from it without contradicting it (s), and to the anthithesis of that which
differs from it without contradicting it (-s).
This may be represented with the proportion: $\dfrac{S \sim s}{-S \sim -s}$

or with the diagramme:

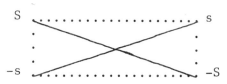

The relationship (S s) or (-S -s) is commonly called an axis; the relationship (S -S) or (s -s) a schema; the relationship (S -s) or (s -S) a deixis (which in one direction is an implication, in the other a presupposition).

The quadrilateral of meaning may be used to illustrate the theology of the Trinity. As I have already done so in a previous publication, I will quote my own text at this point:

> Christian theology speaks of the Father. The meaning of the 'theologeme' /Father/ emerges if one can interpret difference (s) and contradition (-S) in a transcendental way applicable to the being of God. Now, the analogical application of these correlations shows itself with clarity if we posit, as antithetical to the Father, the Son; as different from the Father, the Spirit, who, not being the Father, does nevertheless not stand face to face with him in the schema of contradiction Father-Son; as antithetical to the Spirit, the creatures. This last point may not appear at once. Yet the creatures, being neither the Father nor the Son, belong in the same schema as the Spirit, from whom they differ by the negative sign; they also belong in the same axis as the Son, the axis of filiation; and they are with the Father in a correlation of deixis, for the Father implies them by creation and they evidently presuppose the Father as the Creator.[10]

One may express this in another way. The traditional doctrine of the filiation of the Word from the One whom the early Fathers of the Church, and St Paul himself, called o Theos, perfectly corresponds to the schema (S -S). The doctrine of the spiration of the Third Person from the First corresponds equally well to the axis (S s). The Latin doctrine of the procession ab utroque corresponds to the convergence of the deixis (-S s) with the axis (S s). And the doctrine of creation corresponds to the three-fold relationship of (-s) to (S -S s): creation is implied in the Father as Creator, assumed by the incarnate Logos in his filiation, and evoked in a face to face with the Spirit who, said biblically, "hovers over the face of the abyss" (Gen. 1:2), liturgically, "renovates the face of the earth", and, theologically and experientially, indwells the heart of the faithful.

Comparing our two linguistic approaches, we obtain two converging models. The syntactic line brings attention to the centrality of the Logos as the focus of divine self-revelation. It shows up the Logos as the total expression of the Father and thereby as the supreme participant in the Father's being (homoousios...), whose entire sense is to communicate the divine being, through whom the Father speaks the divine being to the Third Person. Through this Word also the Father speaks the divine being to all creatures, with the necessary accommodations without which creatures would neither be, nor be able to listen and to understand. Such accommodations can easily be identified: God addresses us in prophecy through the medium of human speakers and writers, through the mediation of the Logos incarnate, and through inspiration, which is the assistance and testimony of the Spirit in the heart of those who believe. The syntactic model thus highlights the focus of Trinitarian doctrine.

The semantic model in turn fans out on the entire scope of the horizon of this doctrine. It shows the impossibility of thinking One without the other Two; it indicates the mutual relationships of the Three; it opens the perspective of a "fourth person" in the world of creaturehood, of the created wisdom which images the eternal Wisdom (the Spirit), is assumed in the filiation of the Son, originates from and returns to the fontal fulness of the Father. It thus shows the doctrine and the experience of the Trinity to be the key to the doctrines and the experience of creation, grace, ecclesiology and eschatology.

o o o

This bi-polar linguistic approach may enable us to take a fresh look at some traditional problems. Take, for instance, the question of personhood in God. The classical language, since at least the Cappadocian Fathers, has identified the Three as hypostases or persons. Latin theology, from Boethius through the middle ages,has attempted to refine the definition of personhood in order to make it properly applicable to the divine Three. Several contemporary theologians have endeavored to find better terms than person, in order to avoid the individualistic connotations of the word in some modern languages. Karl Barth has proposed "mode of being". Karl Rahner would prefer "manner of subsisting".[11] And I have myself indicated, in contradiction of this trend, that the principle of personhood is one of the indispensable principles of Trinitarian doctrine.[12] But we deal with three personhoods rather than with three instances of a common personhood. This is precisely what the quadrilateral indicates by placing each person at a distinct intersection of schema, axis and deixis. And it is certainly no improvement to replace the relatively clear term, person, which is rich in human and spiritual experience, by obscure paraphrases like "mode of being" or "manner of subsisting". The problem remains the same with such expressions as with person: each person, or mode, or manner, is not only numerically distinct from the others but also differently structured. The advantage of the quadrilateral at this point is to provide a model to view divine personhood as non-univocal, as differentiated into three types of personhoods.

Or take the vexing problem of the filioque. As the endpoint of the Father-Spirit axis, the Spirit proceeds from the Father alone, as Photius rightly maintained. Yet as belonging to the deixis Word-Spirit, which itself rests on the logically prior schema Father-Word, the Spirit proceeds also through the Son. But this is a different kind of procession: by way of deixis from the Son, over against the procession by way of axis from the Father. This point does not appear in the Augustinian idea that the Spirit proceeds "from both as from one principle".[13] "As from one principle" can only mean that the ultimate origin or principle remains the Father, which, incidentally, is precisely the main concern of the doctrine of Photius. Thus it would seem that the classical Eastern and Western conceptions of the derivation of the Spirit, far from being mutually contradictory, should be reconciled: they bespeak two aspects of the procession of the Third Person.

Finally, the problem of the "fourth person", suggested in the medieval paintings of the coronation of Mary, formulated with some anxiety, though poorly resolved, by Carl Jung,[14] finds its solution in the necessary relationship between the Creator and the creatures. As these come to being from the Father through the Son in the Spirit, they necessarily stand in a threefold relationship to the Three. What is this relationship? The deixis Father-creature denotes the efficient causality of Aristotelian philosophy. The axis, Word-creature, denotes an exemplaristic causality by way of filiation. The schema, Spirit-creature, denotes the final causality, the last end and ultimate purpose of creation. This threefold relationship has left its mark on the many ways in which created reality is experienced under a threefold aspect. Such a threefoldness figures distinctly, if not clearly, in the inner life of the "friends of God", the mystics of all religions. It is at the heart of the experience of the Christian mystics, whose ascent to God reaches its acme with a vivid awareness of participating in the divine processions of the Son and of the Spirit, at the fine point of the soul.

o o o

That the structure of human language provides a contemporary model for understanding and formulating Trinitarian experience and doctrine opens up a complementary perspective. For linguistics itself is a specific case, though the most systematic and elaborate, of human semiotics. To signal

132

something to others, whether in complex systems like the sign language of the deaf or road signalisation, or in spontaneous expressions such as the whimperings of a baby, we set ourselves in a threefold context of coordinates which relate together the self, the other, and the sign between them. Thus a threefold structure of experience already underlies the pre-linguistic or extra-linguistic phase of human life. Anthropologists have identified similar structures in systems of kinship and of social organization, even in the cooking and eating habits of humankind.[15] Investigations of the meaning and nature of temporality, by theologians like St Augustine or philosophers like Jean-Paul Sartre, have noticed the threefoldness of the human sense of time.[16] The irreversibility of time is an image of eternity. On the backdrop of this irreversibility, past, present and future constitute a totality reflected and integrated in the self-consciousness of an "I" which is not only a present, but is still its own past and is already its own future. Between past and future, from memory to hope, the "I" who at the present moment says and acts "I am", says and acts its entire past (and, as Sartre has pointed out in keeping with the doctrine of original sin, a human being is never without a past, for it is born into one). Through this said or acted word the past is proclaimed to the future in which it will be totally integrated as this future becomes present. Out of its memory the self projects its future. Already the intimate structure of the self shows humanity to be unthinkable except within a semiotics which anthropology will call threefold and theology will interpret as Trinitarian.

There used to be a medieval conception, found, for instance, at the heart of Romanesque art, that the key to the universe lies in the self.[17] This key was provided precisely by the proportions of the human body as reflective of spiritual dimensions. For, a point rediscovered by psychoanalysis, the sense of one's inner self feeds one's conscious or unconscious image of one's body. St

Hildegardis of Bingen described the correspondences between the macrocosmos of the universe and the microcosmos of the human body, which she parsed out in seven symbolic sections. Rather than in her pentagrammaton, however, or in the tetragrammaton which the Christian kabbalists of the Renaissance borrowed from Judaism, it is in the pattern of a threefold bodily semiotics that the present self speaks itself as past to itself as future. On the strength of the legs that have carried it from the past into the present, the body breathes and assimilates what is physically needed at the moment, as it anticipates by thought and by the actions of its hands what the future will become. As René Thom's researches into morphogenesis indicate, a "mental image of the body" lies at the origin of psychic activity and, at least hypothetically, at the origin of language and of linguistic and semiotic structures.[18] The integrative function of the image of one's body is confirmed by Jacques Lacan's analyses of the "phase of the mirror" in the development of the child's prehension of the world. Delimitation of and identification with one's body are paradigmatic for social and spiritual integration. Such an image is at the same time quantitative and qualitative. But if a qualitative interpretation of it remains hazardous for philosophical reflection, it becomes clear in the light of Trinitarian faith. The qualitative geography of the body, with the three zones which René Thom calls caudal, ergative and cephalic, implies a logos, an entelechy, in which, the lower serving the higher as the living body passes from the past to the future in space and time, quantity supports and means quality. The living body evolves quantitatively and qualitatively in the time-space continuum to the point where the human self realizes (in the two senses of making and of understanding) its threefold dimension as a past of and from the Father, a present of and through the Son, a future of and in the Spirit. The semiotic dimension of the body, like the symbolic dimension of language, reflects the basic structure of creation in the image of the Three.

134

I am of course aware of the Feuerbachian and Marxist objection or hypothesis, that such a Trinitarian interpretation of basic semiotics shares the fundamental nature of theological propositions: rather than creation being made in the image of a transcendental God, it is the very concept of God which is made by man in the image of himself. The Trinity becomes the heavenly projection, provisionally comforting yet gratuitous and ultimately deleterious, of human hopes; and these hopes result from the catastrophic effects on the human psyche of the dehumanizing conditions of work brought about by individual ownership of the means of production. Admittedly, the imaging relationship of the self and the divine Three works two ways. Like Jacob's ladder where angels descend and ascend, the constructive activity of the mind can imagine the Three on the basis of a discerned threefoldness in human life, as theological reflection can also,on the basis of what the Christian tradition has taught about the Three, reinterpret the human experience. St Augustine was well aware of this when he investigated the psychological analogy of the Trinity. Typology proceeds from the signifying typos to the signified antitypos and back again. Symbolization is a double-edged sword. So Feuerbach and Marx are not notably vulnerable in their hypothesis. Their weak line is the inference that the existence of an ascending movement by which God is imagined on a human pattern effectively rules out a descending movement by which the human is imaged on a divine model. The hypothesis that such a descending pattern does exist independently of the ascending model is scientifically as respectable as the hypothesis of its non-existence. Further, if one admits the philosophically inescapable principle that the universe must ultimately make sense, the positive hypothesis is intellectually more satisfactory and practically more useful than the negative. There of course remains a gap between this statement and the certainty of faith that the Three divine Persons known as Father, Word, Spirit, are the origin, the model, and the purpose of all that is. Humanly speaking, this gap calls for risking the leap of

135

faith. Theologically, it is filled by the gift of faith.

Yet there is a further challenge in Trinitarian faith. If this faith is indeed "practically useful", one should carefully determine what praxis follows from it. This is all the more important as it is at the level of praxis that much contemporary thinking, following Marx's theses on Feuerbach, gauges the worth of ideas. Precisely at this level, Trinitarian thought has a long experience of human praxis. Not only in language has Trinitarian faith been expressed. In La Théologie parmi les sciences humaines[19] I have pointed out that theology can and does use other media. Esthetic experience, in the great periods of religious art, has been a means of both theological expression and theological perception. The Trinitarian aspect of esthetic experience was pointed out above in the case of Romanesque art. It can also be seen as effectively informing Gothic art and Oriental iconography. Several lines in fact converge at this point: the line that we followed through early Christian art, when popular decorative motifs of sarcophagi acted as a means of holding and expressing Trinitarian faith; the line of the mystical experience of the Three expressed poetically, when poetry is itself intrinsic to the mystic's openness to the threefold gift of divine grace, as in the works of John of the Cross; the New Testament line, where the Trinity is neither revealed as a transcendental truth to be believed, nor directly apprehended and accepted as a doctrine, but presented as a recurring vision. Indeed, it is the very theme and thesis of the present book that such a recurring vision is the key to everything in heaven and on earth.

The Trinitarian vision is the key to esthetics. Dorothy Sears explored this in The Mind of the Maker:[20] she detected the Trinitarian dimension of the creative process at work in the praxis of the artist. One could indeed pursue this perspective at two levels. First, at the level of the esthetic expression of Trinitarian faith. When Gerald Man-

ley Hopkins, in <u>The Wreck of the Deutschland</u>
(1875), wrote of

...God, three-numbered form...
...Mid-numbered He in three of the thunder-
throne...

did language provide a form to his previously
given faith? Or, as with John of the Cross, did
not his experience of the Three mold his use of
language so that the Trinity was truly the "inscape" of his verses?   Similar questions may be
asked in reference to other arts.   When Andrei
Rublev paints his famous icon of the philoxenia
of Abraham, he does more than express theological
ideas in a plastic medium, although he does this
too: he experiences the Three in the vision which
appears as his brush strokes transform the surface
of the wood.   When Olivier Messiaen composes his
<u>Meditations sur le mystère de la Sainte Trinité</u> to
be played on the organ, he not only puts together
a musical theology of the Trinity; he also experiences the Three Persons through the medium of
organ music.   The praxis of the painter for Rublev, that of the organist for Messiaen, are in
their own context what John of the Cross calls, in
an auditive-linguistic analogy, "substantial locutions".   These are bestowed by God "in order to
accomplish Himself what they express".[21] What they
express is more or less grasped; but what they accomplish is fully effected.   Here, expression and
fulfilment are one.   <u>Theoria</u> and <u>praxis</u> coincide
in God's own creative <u>fiat</u>.

But a second level is suggested by the first.
Can we not think that, in some sense, every
esthetic experience, whatever the medium and whatever one's mode of involvement – whether as creative artist or as seeking on-looker – participates, though ever so faintly, in the experience
of the Three?   This would be in keeping with artists' frequent impression of working under the
influence of a <u>daimon</u>, of responding to a muse's
call (see the: <u>Poête, prends ton luth and me donne
un baiser...in Alfred de Musset's Nuit de mai</u>).   It

would correspond also to the detachment of many artists once the deed has been done, the canvas painted, the melody composed, the poem written. These are no longer their work; in a sense they never were. The artists were prophets of a vision which escaped them as it transformed them. In turn, the on-looker, the contemplative, enters a new spiritual world through the poem read, the painting seen, the symphony heard. Interested by-standers who approach a "thing of beauty" become caught in it. They find themselves humming the melody, following the strokes on the canvas as though painting it, repeating words heard or read as though testing their evocative power. The on-looker becomes a creative artist, perceiving new dimensions of reality. Having entered a museum as actor, the visitor leaves as acted upon by the vision perceived. The pilgrim has been carried to the goal of comprehension. The viator has become comprehensor. The novice has received enlightenment. Yet such a process is no other, at a qualitatively high level, than imaging the Three Persons through the space-time experience inscribed in the formation of one's body-image.

That the theological tradition, since Augustine, has extensively explored the analogies of love to explain Trinitarian doctrine derives from a fundamental intuition that, of all human experiences, the experience of love constitutes a privileged context for aiming at the Trinity. Trinitarian faith is an experience before being a teaching, a vision before being a formulation. And this vision is felt and acted no less than seen. It is an experiential vision in which all spiritual and bodily senses participate even though unawares. Here indeed, seeing is believing; but doing is seeing. This I attempted to show in A Way of Love: "To know God as One-in-Three is to experience that God's love is not a metaphor but a reality, the ultimate reality."22 But experience of God's love is not reserved to the contemplative who, through mystical purifications, is brought face to face with the divine Persons in their full reality. Already it is experienced by those who,

138

at the level of human relationships, have found their life and their being fulfilled in the love of another. Every human loving and being loved places us on the path to the vision of the Three, in that it makes us share some aspect or element or dimension of this vision. Awareness of unity-in-distinction among human persons reflects the unity-in-distinction of the divine Persons. If God is love and the Trinity may be understood as a relationship in love, then every love in the created world is also Trinitarian.[23] The mystery of God as One and Three comes, as it were, to our level when, in human love, one obtains the experience of being both onself and another, a self speaking and giving itself to another, who in turn speaks and gives itself to the first. In such an experience, there are three: the self, and the other, and the "we" of their union. The Father differentiates himself from his self-expression as Other - his Word - as he addresses himself to the one who, as their mutual and common "We", is called their Spirit. This is, admittedly, another analogy than those which were explored by St Augustine or by Richard of St Victor. In the twelfth-century monastic context of Richard, and given the personal history of Augustine, the analogy of love had to come from psychological and intellectual analysis rather than from the experience of human love. While these analyses remain valid at their level, they need to be complemented by an analogy founded in the praxis of love in which human persons are raised above themselves into the spiritual community of their union.

The experience of love and its purifying effect on human life inspire what may be called an esthetics of life. In La Théologie parmi les sciences humaines I have drawn attention to the fact that theology is not only spoken in language and expressed in the manifold semiotics of art, but can also be lived and thus inscribed in flesh and blood. This may be seen with some degree of evidence in the lives of saints. But the esthetics of life is also at work in ordinary human relationships dominated by love, whether the love between man and woman, or the love of friends, or the love of neighbor which is aroused when another brings us assistance, or the universal compassion which conditions the search for justice and sets the context for love. The analysis of love made in A Way of Love shows several ways in which the esthetics of life, like the esthetics of art, serves as symbol of the Three Persons and as means to enter here and now into the divine life.

Yet the present conditions of the world seem to raise an additional question, as they provide a darkening background to the vision of the Three. Can the organization of the city, the political order, the structures of society, so participate in the esthetics of life that they themselves become symbols of the divine interrelationships? The contemporary deterioration of society suggests, by contrast, dreams of utopia. But can the Christian utopia of today become the reality of tomorrow? In final analysis, this is the question raised, if not answered, by the theologies of liberation. It may well be that the experience of the third world, struggling for love through justice, contributing the gift of each tradition and nation to the civilization of the universal, courageously attempting to build an order in which both individuals and societies can receive according to their needs and produce according to their capacities, will eventually provide a more collective symbolization of and participation in the divine life. I am admittedly skeptical as to the historical possibility of such a development. But one may not rule out that some day the vision of the Three may be perceived by all humankind, when a "we" spoken by all humanity will image the Father speaking the Word in and to the Spirit.

1. On the Koran as divine Word, see R.C. Zaehner: The Comparison of Religions, New York, 1962, p.199. In Hinduism, the Katha-upanishad declares: "He (the Self) cannot be reached by speech, by mind, or by the eye. How can it be apprehended except by him who says: He is?" (Katha-upanishad II, 6 valli, 12) in Max Müller, tr.: The Upanishads Sacred Books of the East, XV) vol. II, New York, 1962, p. 23.

2. I am thinking here especially of José Miranda's view, that the proper translation of John 1:1 is "the Word was addressed to God" (Being and the Messiah. The Message of St. John, Maryknoll, N.Y., 1977, p. 121). This is of course gramatically possible. Yet it makes little sense, for it would conceal the identity of the speaker.

3. La Théologie parmi les sciences humaines, Paris, 1975.

4. Op. cit., p. 82.

5. D.-S., 1330. Admittedly, to speak of a relation of opposition is in keeping with traditional language. Thomas Aquinas writes, for instance: De ratione relationis est respectus unius ad alterum, secundum quem aliquid alteri opponitur relative ("The relationship of one to another, insofar as a thing is relatively opposed to another, belongs to the nature of relation", S. Th., I, q. 28, a. 3). I also used similar language above, p. 71-74. Here, however, I wish to make the point that in God neither relation nor opposition is to be taken in an antagonistic sense. In Mao Zedong's vocabulary, the "opposition" of relation" in God is a "non-antagonistic contradiction" rather than an "antagonistic contradiction" (Mao-tse-tung: On Contradiction, p. 68-71, in Four Essays on Philosophy, Peking, 1968).

6. Ascent of Mount Carmel, II, 22, 5, op. cit., p. 180.

7. J. L. Austin: How to Do Things with Words, Cambridge, Mass., 1962.

8. One may consult such classics as Vladimir Propp: Morphology of the Folktale, 2nd ed., Austin, 1968; A. J. Greimas: Du Sens, Essais sémiotiques, Paris, 1970, esp. p. 157-83: "Eléments d'une grammaire narrative."

9. Ferdinand de Saussure: Cours de linguistique générale, Paris, 1961; Louis Hjelmslev, op. cit., n. 13-4; Greimas, op. cit., p. 39-48; 135-55; Sémantique structurale, Paris, 1966.

10. op. cit., p. 65.

11. Karl Barth: Church Dogmatics, I/1, Edinburgh, 1975, p. 355-66.

12. See above, ch. III, p. 74-78.

13. See above, ch. III, note 17.

14. See above, ch. III, note 4.

15. Claude Lévi-Strauss: The Elementary Structures of Kinship, Boston, 1969; The Raw and the Cooked, New York, 1969.

16. St Augustine: The Confessions, bk XII ch. 11-31, op. cit., p. 252-69; Jean-Paul Sartre: L'Etre et le Néant, part II, ch. 2, Paris, 1976, p. 145-89. The following analysis untersects with Rahner's identification of the two processions as one self-communication having the two aspects of origin and future (op. cit., p. 88-99). But there remains a significant difference, in that Rahner relates origin to the Second Person, whereas I see origin as symbolic of the First Person, the "fontal fulness" of all that is.

17. Marie-Madeleine Davy: Initiation à la symbolique romane, Paris, 1964; on St Hildegardis, see ibidem, p. 163-71.

18. René Thom: Modèles mathématiques de la morphogenèse, Paris, 1974. See Jacques Lacan: Le Stade du miroir comme formateur de la fonction du Je, in

Ecrits, vol. I, Paris, 1966, p. 90-97.

19. Especially p. 90-94.

20. *The Mind of the Maker*, London, 1942.

21. *Ascent of Mount Carmel*, II, 31, 2, op. cit., p. 210-211.

22. *A Way of Love*, New York, 1977, p. 131; see also *Meditation on the Word*, New York, 1968, p. 129-69.

23. This explains the Trinitarian symbolism of my poetry, in Henri Wasser: *La Septième Vague*, Paris, 1976; *Song for Avalokita*, Philadelphia, 1979.

CONCLUSION

I have been well aware, while writing this book, of the difficulty of selling the idea that the Trinity should be the central concern of theology today. A series of factors seem to militate against this view: the recent stress of New Testament research upon the human Jesus, the anthropological shift of theological reflection, the popularization of images of Christ as the Man-for-others or as the Liberator of the oppressed, the growing sensitivity of Christians to the insights of other religions, the feeling that, like philosophers since Karl Marx, theologians ought to change the world rather than explain it...The ensuing atmosphere is not a good conductor for the thesis I am proposing.

One can also formulate more specific objections. The vision of the Three by artists through the ages has derived from individual dreams and projects, even when the art itself by its location in public places has served the purposes of corporate worship. But the accent today is not - and probably should not be - on the individual. Those who immerse themselves in the masses, those who work for the masses, seem to be riding the wave of the future. What need do we then have of individual visions? Likewise, the mystics' experience has always been personal and interior, never duplicated. It has been a quintessential appropriation of something which by right should have belonged to all, yet has not been shared by all. But if there may well be individual mystics among us who go on following their personal ascent, the call today both in the church and in the secular world is to inspire peoples and nations, to shape collectivities. If it is granted that the Three of the Trinity are a society of its own very special kind, we now live in a society of billions of people, to which it is impossible to present a society of three as an ideal.

All this is certainly true. It is obviously true. But the art of reading the signs of the times does not reside in highlighting the obvious. It is to perceive the signs that are not obvious, that have hardly begun to emerge, whose shape is not yet delineated. There is no need to ask the watchman: "What of the night?" when everyone can see the rising of the moon. And it can happen that the obvious signs of the times hide the less clear. Yet the strength of the obvious signs may already be spent, while the key to the future lies with the more hidden.

I have alluded at various places to such hidden signs in the general area of linguistics and semiotics (the science of signs). The very structure of meaning seems to rest on a structure of reality of which one cannot decide for certain whether it be bi-focal or tri-focal. Hence the union, in the anthropological analyses of Claude Lévi-Strauss, of two basic models for society, a dual model on the male-female pattern and a three-fold model on the pattern of raw-rotten-cooked in eating habits. Predominance of a three-fold model seems to carry conviction, if one notices, with Lévi-Strauss, that the very structure of human societies is to make possible the necessary exchanges between two groups. Exchange requires threeness, since the two are united in what they exchange. One finds a similar wavering between the two and the three in Jacques Lacan's interpretation of Freud. Even the Marxist division of society between the have's and the have-not's, the capitalists and the proletarians, has been considerably modified by Mao Zedong's analysis of contradictions: besides a distinction between non-antagonistic and antagonistic contradictions (the latter corresponding to the two poles of the class struggle in Marx), Mao introduces consideration of a principal aspect of the contradiction over against its secondary aspects.[1] But the secondary aspects have introduced a third element which is irreducible either to the principal aspect or to any of the two poles of the contradiction. Even if Mao Zedong did not exploit this insight fully, he has effectively broken Marx's dualism.

What do such things prove? They prove nothing-yet. But we may soon have to return to Simone Weil, the first and still the greatest theologian of liberation. "Equilibrium," she wrote, "is the proportional means between gravity and non-gravity. Justice is the proportional means between spiritual freedom and force."[2] Simone Weil was strongly Trinitarian in her religion, as perusal of her Journals shows manifestly. She found intimations of the Trinity in Greek literature and mythology, in the Upanishads, in esthetics, in mathematics, in the sciences. The method of social analysis with which she wanted to replace that of Marx was founded on a trilogy: the poles of thought and action are the two ways in which human being lives and makes progress. "True freedom is not defined by a relation between desire and satisfaction, but by a relation between thought and action."[3] She criticized Marxism precisely because, as "the highest spiritual expression of bourgeois society," it thinks only in the dual terms of the class struggle which was created by bourgeois society. But the solution of oppression is spiritual struggle, not civil war: "There are not two methods of social architecture. There is only one. It is eternal. But it is always the eternal which demands from the human spirit a true effort at invention. It consists in disposing the blind forces of social mechanics around the point which is also the center of the blind forces of the heavenly mechanics, that is, "the Love which moves the sun and the other stars"..."[4] Between the opposite dimensions inherent in oppression (the oppressor and the oppressed), one must insert a third dimension: "If one looks carefully, not only at the Christian Middle Ages but also at all truly creative civilizations, one notices that in each of them, at least for a time, there was at the very center an empty place reserved to the purely supernatural, to the reality located outside this world. Everything else was turned toward this empty place."[5] The oppressor who is concerned about this center ceases to oppress, and the oppressed ceases to hate the oppressor. For relation to what is spiritual is effected in prayer. And Simone Weil proposes the following rule: "There is no other perfect criterion of good and evil than uninterrupted interior prayer. All is allowed which does not interrupt it, nothing is allowed of what interrupts it. It is impossible to hurt another when one acts in a state of prayer. On condition that it be true prayer." [6] Simone Weil well knew the Trinitarian context and structure of prayer.

That the human striving for liberation results from a fundamental experience of the divine Three is far from evident to the contemporary practitioners of revolution. Following Marx, many take it for granted that all religious ideas and practices are enemies of the revolution, tools of oppression. But it was not always so. In fact utopias proposed at various times as ideals for a new society have been strongly tainted with Trinitarianism. Montanism and Joachimism are cases in point. Only with the Renaissance have utopias — like that of St Thomas More — been detached from their traditional ties with the doctrine of the Holy Spirit. With some exceptions, as in the works of Rosemary Ruether and in some writings of José Miranda, the recent theologies of liberation have been exclusively oriented toward christology, proposing the image of Christ as the leader of the true exodus, as the Liberator. But Christ has no lasting meaning unless in connection with the Father and the Spirit. The doctrine of the Trinity, as I have tried to show, finds its depth in the fact that it is primarily a vision. Only a vision can awaken the hopes that lie dormant in the human soul. Only a vision can lead humankind to a really new future.

1. Mao Tse-tung: _Four Essays on Philosophy_, Peking, 1966, p. 51-59; 79-95.

2. Simone Weil: _Cahiers_, vol. 3, Paris, 1956, p. 145.

3. _Cahiers_, vol. 3, p. 117.

4. _Oppression et Liberté_, Paris, 1955, p. 174.

5. _Oppression et Liberté_, p. 219.

6. _Cahiers_, vol. 3, p. 145.

Index of names

Index of subjects

154

eucharist   50
exemplarism   123

faith   38-40, 44, 50
Father, God the   33-46, 58, 69-70, 103-104,
                      111-112, 127
filioque   72, 75, 82, 130-133

God as love   46, 102, 119
gothic art   40-44, 137
grammar   120-127

hesychasm   73, 97
Hinduism   57, 97, 142
Holy Scripture   53-54, 64, 98, 122-123
Holy Spirit   23, 35-38, 42, 72-73, 102-104,
                  111, 126-127, 139
homoousios   35-38, 46, 62-64, 67-71, 130
humanity of Christ   24, 99-100, 145

iconoclasm   52
icons   47-52, 137-138
immanence   44
immanent Trinity   84, 98-99
infancy narratives   16-17
Ishvara   95, 97
Islam   81, 95-96, 119, 125

Joachimism   148
Johannine gospel   2, 18-19, 122
Judaism   1-3, 59, 81, 119, 125, 135
judeo-christians   59, 61

knowledge of God   93, 136
Kyrios   11, 33, 59
Krishna   95
kingdom   9-11

language   123-131, 135, 137
liberation   145, 148
liberator   145, 148
light   49, 67, 85-86, 104, 113
linguistics   121-122, 129-133, 134, 146
liturgy   44, 50, 93-95, 145
Logos   17, 33-34, 63, 66, 68, 119-124, 130
love   77, 80, 89, 101-103, 119, 138-139